Dec-2013

ADVICE FROM A BROAD ABROAD

TayTay,

I met the author of this book in September 2013 at a work event. This is written specifically for women travelers. It is full of advice and is supposed to be a good read. I hope you find it helpful as you embark on your next chapter in London. I wish you all the best and know you'll love it. I'll come visit as much as possible.

Merry Christmas,
Graham

LAURETTA ANN REEVES

Copyright © 2013 Lauretta Ann Reeves

All rights reserved.

ISBN: 1484990854

ISBN 13: 9781484990858

Library of Congress Control Number: 2013909630
CreateSpace Independent Publishing Platform
North Charleston, South Carolina

CONTENTS

Chapter 1: Travel and the Job Interview 1
    Quick Guide 1
    Preparing for Interviews 1
    Discussing Travel Early in the Interview Process 2
        Minimal Interest in Traveling 2
        Eager to Travel 2
    Reconciling Travel Expectations and Your Lifestyle 3
    Discussing Travel Late in the Interview Process 4

Chapter 2: Travel and Your New Job 5
    Quick Guide 5
    Find Out the Rules 5
    Select/Interview a Travel Agent 6
    Construct a Travel Profile 7
    Review Insurance Needs 8
        Life/Disability Insurance/Long-Term-Care Insurance 8
        Health Insurance 8
    Consider Emergency Travel Assistance 8

Chapter 3: Family and Home Preparation 11
    Quick Guide 11
    Separation Anxiety 11
    Home Preparation 12

Chapter 4: Travel Basics 13
    Quick Guide 13
    Passports 13

New Passports and Passport Card	13
Expedited Passports	14
Expired Passports	14
Lost Passports	15
E-Passports	15
Hotel and Airline Programs	15
Airline Clubs	17
Credit/Debit Cards	17
Credit Cards	17
Debit Cards	18
Other Cards	19
Phone Cards	19
AAA Card	19
AARP Card	19
Business Cards	20
Trusted Traveler Programs	20
Global Entry Program	20
TSA Precheck-√™	21

Chapter 5: Trip Construction ... 23

Quick Guide	23
Determining the Duration	23
Refining the Focus/Filling in the Schedule	24
Maximizing Your Budget	25
Travel around the World	25
Travel on Off-Peak Days or Seasons	26
Compare Airline Fares	27
Consider Alternate Ports of Entry	27
Travel in Coach	27
Travel in Economy Plus	27
Travel by Train	28
Book Ahead	28
Look for Specials	28
Prepay for Travel	28
Obtaining Travel Documents	29
Passports	29
Visas	29

Chapter 6: **Pretravel Checkup** 31
   Quick Guide 31
   Checkups 31
      Vaccinations *32*
   Flying Acclimation 33

Chapter 7: **Travel Wardrobe, Luggage, and Toiletries** 35
   Quick Guide 35
   Travel Wardrobe 35
      Weather Considerations *36*
      Minimum Essentials *36*
      Color Coordination *36*
      Value Shopping *36*
      Shoe Selection *37*
   Luggage 38
      Garment Bags Versus Rollaboards *38*
      Luggage Color *38*
   Computer Bags 38
   Cosmetics/Toiletries 39
      Double-Duty Cosmetics *39*
      Sample-Size Makeup and Containers *39*
      Cosmetic Brushes *40*
      Other Products *40*

Chapter 8: **Travel Electronics** 41
   Quick Guide 41
   Business Electronics 41
      IT Advice *41*
      Wireless Cards/Cellular *42*
      Adaptors and Cables *42*
      Card Scanners *43*
   Personal Electronics 43
      Headphones *43*
      Electronic Books *44*
      Personal Digital Assistants *44*
      Smartphones *45*
      Netbooks, iPads, Touch-Screen Tablets *46*
      Curling Irons *47*

    Hairdryers *47*
  Safeguarding 47
    Public Use *47*
    Engraving *47*
    Highlighting *48*
    Register *48*
    Store Data *48*
    Enable Tracking Programs *48*
    Helpful Apps *48*

Chapter 9: **Foreign Languages and Cultures** 51
  Quick Guide 51
  Self-Taught Language Courses 52
    Foreign Language Institute *52*
    Pimsleur Approach *52*
    Learn in Your Car *52*
    In-Flight *53*
  Culture 53
    China *53*
    Japan *54*
    India *55*
    Russia *55*
    Saudi Arabia *56*
    France *57*
    Germany *57*
    Italy *57*
    Spain *58*
    United Kingdom *58*
    Argentina *59*
    Brazil *59*
    Venezuela *60*
    South Africa *60*

Chapter 10: **Itinerary Creation** 61
  Quick Guide 61
  Plotting Your Itinerary 61
  Mapping Your Itinerary 62
  Selecting Airplane Seats 63

Selecting a Seatmate	63
Selecting the Zone	64
Selecting the Level	64
Selecting the Row	64
Selecting the Seat	65
Confirming and Changing Seats	65

Chapter 11: **Preweek Preparations** 67
Quick Guide	67
Assess the Weather	67
Select the Proper Clothes	68
Obtain Medicines and Toiletries	68
Forward Documents	68
Copy Passport Pages	69
Copy Wallet Contents	70
Back Up the Hard Drive	70

Chapter 12: **Preday Preparation** 71
Quick Guide	71
Confirm Your Itinerary	71
Print Your Boarding Pass	72
Check the Weather	72
Packing	72
Packing Suit Carriers (Lightly)	72
Packing Rollaboards and Computer Bags	73
ID Your Belongings	75
Forwarding Luggage	75

Chapter 13: **Final Preparations** 77
Quick Guide	77
Reconfirm Your Flights	77
Check the Essentials	77
Zip and Button	78
Hug Your Loved Ones	78

Chapter 14: **Airport Considerations** 79
Quick Guide	79
Check In	79
Passport Control and Security	80

Chapter 15: **Safety and Convenience** 83
   Quick Guide 83
   At the Hotel 83
      Room Escort *83*
      Room Entrance *84*
      Evacuation Route *84*
      Emergency Lighting *84*
      Proper Unpacking *84*
      Visitor Checks *85*
      Night Preparation *85*
      Securing Valuables *85*
   Outside the Hotel 86
      Carrying Important Items *86*
      Filing a "Flight Plan" *86*
      Traveling Safely *86*
      Monitoring Valuables *87*
      Using Toilets *87*
      Tipping Properly *88*

Chapter 16: **Healthy Traveling** 89
   Quick Guide 89
   Eat Well 89
   Exercise Frequently 90
   Rest Sufficiently 92
   Stay Clean 92
   Avoid Infectious Diseases 93
      Food-borne and Waterborne Diseases *93*
      Other Infectious Diseases *93*

Chapter 17: **Roaming Abroad** 95
   Quick Guide 95
   Intercity 95
      Planes *95*
      Trains *96*
      Rental Cars *97*
   Intracity . . . .
      Trains/Metro/Subways/Buses *98*
      Taxis *98*
      On Foot *99*

Chapter 18: **Other Travel Considerations** 101
- Quick Guide 101
- Safeguarding Business Documents 101
- Common Courtesies 102
  - *Canceled/Postponed Flights* *103*
  - *Airport Closures* *103*
- Savoring Downtime 104
  - *Take a Walk* *104*
- Visit a Museum, the Zoo or a Park 105
- Schedule a Tour 105
- Preparing for Customs and Immigration 106
  - *Immigration Forms* *106*
  - *Prohibited Items* *106*
  - *Customs* *106*

Chapter 19: **Trip Recovery** 107
- Quick Guide 107
- Acclimate Your Body 107
- Celebrate Your Homecoming 108
- Unpack and Take Inventory 108
- Retrieve Lost Articles 108
  - *Back Up Your Computer* *109*
  - *Trip Follow-up* *109*
  - *Complete Your Expense Report* *109*
  - *Reinforce New Contacts* *110*
- Save Your Photographs 110
- Plan Your Next Trip 110

SANTORINI, GREECE

CHAPTER 1: **TRAVEL AND THE JOB INTERVIEW**

> **QUICK GUIDE**
> - Research your potential employers
> - Prepare your questions
> - Determine your travel limitations and expectations
> - Understand your employer's travel expectations and benefits

Preparing for Interviews

The interview process is very important to both the employer and the prospective employee. Preparing for your interviews is crucial to finding and landing the job you really want. If a career coach is not in your budget, there are many websites, such as CVTips.com, that offer pointers. Career coaches suggest you carefully research the prospective company, analyze the job description, familiarize yourself with various types of interviews, display passion during the interview process, and end the interview strongly. These are all important parts of landing the job you want.

But are you sure you want the job you might be offered? Interviews are a two-way street. This is your chance to have the companies define their expectations so you can compare what different companies can offer *you!*

Discussing Travel Early in the Interview Process

Before you walk into each interview, prepare a list of questions that will help you compare job offers and impress the interviewer with your preparation. Going beyond the size of your potential office and benefits, you should explore whether a company's values are consistent with yours.

As companies expand globally—sourcing, selling, building, and hiring abroad—the demand for itinerant professionals will increase. As a professional woman changing jobs or entering the workforce, you might be required to travel. In preparing for your interview, it would be wise to consult with several colleagues or friends (preferably women) working in your target field for interview advice and information on job expectations and travel requirements.

Minimal Interest in Traveling

If traveling is not your interest, don't initiate a discussion about it during your interviews, but don't dismiss a job outright if it appears frequent journeys will be a requirement. Instead, ask for details on the frequency and type of travel, or mention you may need time or assistance arranging for family needs. Consider carefully the firm's responses during your decision making.

Eager to Travel

If you are eager to explore the world, ask these questions early in the process:

- Does the position for which you are applying, or others on your potential career path in the firm, involve travel?
- What is the typical duration of these trips?
- How often are you expected to be on the road?
- How much notice do you receive before you travel?
- What are the percentages of domestic and international travel?
- Does the company have a dedicated travel department, or are employees expected to fend for themselves?

TRAVEL AND THE JOB INTERVIEW

Later in this chapter and in the next, you will find questions to pose to your firm's travel agent and accounting office either after you have been hired or during your decision phase.

Reconciling Travel Expectations and Your Lifestyle

You need to reconcile the answers to these questions with your expectations for your lifestyle. When you're traveling, do you have a spouse, relative, friend, or institutional-care setting that can take care of your children, cats, dogs, and other dependents? Is the company willing to offer this support for short and long trips? How much advance notice do your caregivers require?

How else do you spend your free time? How much will your travel interfere with your ability to continue pursuing your hobbies and enjoying other parts of your life? Will the experiences and career advancement you gain by traveling be worth the sacrifices you make to do so?

My travel experiences have been worth the sacrifices, but I had to make hard choices as I advanced in my career. Working as an institutional trader, my occasional travel interfered little with pursuing my master's degree. As an international stock analyst, I integrated studying for the Chartered Financial Analyst (CFA) designation as I traveled more frequently domestically and abroad.

Moving up the career ladder to become portfolio manager/director of research at a new firm—and eventually co-chief investment officer—required frequent travel and hard decisions. My husband didn't want to take care of babies while I was flying all over the place, so we decided to forgo kids (although we did adopt cats and dogs). For a while, I decided not to pursue further education or even piano lessons. When I was home, I had enough challenges keeping up with housework, my job, and my marriage to want any other obligations.

For me it was worth it. As I became more comfortable traveling abroad, I enjoyed visiting new places, experiencing exotic cultures, trying new foods, and meeting new friends and colleagues. I accumulated frequent-flyer and hotel points that allowed me to take my travel-challenged husband on vacations in the United States and abroad, to places I would not have had the resources, courage, or interest to visit without having fulfilled the travel requirements of my job.

In addition, the knowledge gained while traveling abroad made me a more valuable resource to my firm, and my husband was able to retire and focus on our growing domestic zoo. Eventually, I was able to start piano and voice lessons and continue traveling.

My decision to take a job that involved an increasing amount of travel was the right one for me. You need to decide if it's right for you.

Discussing Travel Late in the Interview Process

Let's suppose you're ready to take on the challenges and excitement of traveling abroad. Consider asking these questions as you choose between positions and negotiate your terms of employment:

- ➢ Will I have flexibility in choosing when I travel, or is it on demand?
- ➢ Does the company make any provisions for dependents (children, incapacitated parents, pets) when I travel?
- ➢ Do I receive additional compensation if I have to travel on weekends or holidays?
- ➢ Will I be able to keep all frequent-flyer, hotel, and rental-car points?
- ➢ May I choose the airlines, hotels, or car rental agencies?
- ➢ Under what circumstances may I upgrade to a better class for flights, hotel rooms, or cars?
- ➢ Will I be given per diem (set amount per day) or reimbursed on the amounts actually spent?

These are questions best explored toward the end of the recruitment and negotiating process. The next chapter will present questions for after you have been hired.

PARIS, FRANCE

CHAPTER 2: **TRAVEL AND YOUR NEW JOB**

> **QUICK GUIDE**
> - Interview your firm's travel administrator or agent
> - Construct a travel profile
> - Review your insurance needs
> - Consider travel assistance

Find Out the Rules

Many corporations have strict rules regarding scheduling trips and reimbursement for expenses. You may have covered some of these questions in your interview, but it's still important to review the rules with whoever signs the reimbursement checks or administers travel. Some questions to pose:

> ➤ Are employees reimbursed on a per diem basis (unusual in international travel, but still possible), or are there maximum amounts that one is reimbursed for hotel rooms or food?

- Does the firm reimburse for miscellaneous airline expenses, such as checked bags, onboard food, and Internet?
- Who completes the expense reports? Are there instructions on how to do so?
- What is the minimum expense for which you don't need a receipt?
- Are firm or personal credit cards used to make reservations?
- Are there different rules for different types of travel (i.e., corporate versus marketing)?
- Can the traveler deviate from corporate hotels if the person is willing to pay the difference in cost?
- Is there an annual travel budget?
- Does all travel have to be made through one person or through an agency?
- Are there specific hotels and airlines with which the firm has alliances?
- When can you book business and first class instead of economy?
- Does the traveler or the firm keep airline miles and hotel points?
- Is there a minimum and maximum time period for each international trip?
- Can personal travel be linked to business travel, and are significant others permitted along on trips?
- Are there limitations on the number of employees reserved for the same flight or train?
- Who preapproves travel?

Select/Interview a Travel Agent

Depending on your firm's rules, you may be able to book most of your flights, hotels, and car rentals online. International travel, however, can be very complicated, and you will want someone you can trust to help you out when you're five thousand miles and six time zones away. If the firm has not designated an agent, international travelers should find a professional travel provider—perhaps a local agent whom colleagues have used, your credit card travel-service provider, or AAA. Try out the agent on some simple domestic trips before you hire him or her for complicated, international travel.

TRAVEL AND YOUR NEW JOB

A travel agent can make the difference between your business travel being hell or heaven, so it's a good idea for all interested parties—you, the agent, and your assistant—to meet, preferably in person but at least over the phone.

Construct a Travel Profile

Your travel agent may already have a profile form on which you can note your preferences. Fill it out as soon as possible so you can sleep at your preferred hotel rather than Bob's Rooms down the street. If your agent doesn't have a prepared form, make your own and give her a copy. Preprinted or self-prepared, items that you want on this form include:

- Your full name (as shown on your passport or other ID), your cell phone number, and emergency contact.

- A list of airlines in descending order of preference, along with your frequent-flyer numbers and associated elite status.

- The preferred seating arrangement when flying, e.g., window or aisle (can't think of one reason anyone would want a middle seat), bulkhead or not, front or back of the plane, and preference regarding exit-row seats. Exit-row seats offer more legroom, but they may not recline.

- The list of hotel chains and respective account numbers in descending order of preference, and any associated elite status.

- Preferences for the type and location of hotel rooms. I like rooms on high floors away from elevators; someone with ambulatory difficulties might prefer the opposite. A former colleague refuses to stay in tall hotels in earthquake-prone areas. This is not something a travel agent would normally consider, so make sure the agent knows all your preferences.

- The preferred list of rental car agencies, along with any club numbers, and your auto preferences. For instance, at a height of not quite five foot two, I prefer a midsize vehicle so I can reach the brakes. In addition, I don't drive a stick shift with any grace whatsoever, so I prefer an automatic transmission. This last requirement is especially important, as it's difficult to rent automatic transmissions internationally.

- After assuring the security of your information, provide it with your primary and backup credit card numbers, passport number, and driver's license number.

Your travel agent must have a copy of your firm's travel rules. Also, ascertain the agency's special arrangements, if any, with certain hotels and airlines.

Unfortunately, mistakes can happen.

Before the days when passengers had to show boarding passes, take off their shoes, dump their computers and jackets on a conveyor belt, and walk through a metal detector, I once made it all the way to my departing gate before discovering my tickets were for a different day. Luckily there was room on the flight, and the agent welcomed me on board.

More recently, a travel agent booked nonrefundable Eurostar train tickets. My schedule changed and the nonrefundable tickets were useless. With only hours to plan a new way to get from Paris to London, I paid three hundred dollars to get a train that night.

It's important to document all your requests, and changes in requests, with your travel agent.

Review Insurance Needs

Life/Disability Insurance/Long-Term-Care Insurance

If you have a spouse or dependents, make sure you have adequate insurance in case something unfortunate happens. Check with your employer to see if the company provides sufficient life, disability, and long-term-care insurance or workman's compensation in case you are unable to work following an accident. Make sure the policies apply to your travels abroad. If your current insurance is insufficient, try to augment your coverage with your employer at a discount, or with one of your other insurance carriers.

Health Insurance

Most medical policies require that you use an "in-network" physician, which could be a challenge when traveling abroad. Before you travel, locate a list of physicians you can contact in your destination cities or countries. Often these can be found on the Internet.

Consider Emergency Travel Assistance

In the case of most travel interruptions, you can simply rebook your flight through your carrier or contact your travel agent, most of whom offer (expensive) after-hours assistance. For severe instances, such as political upheaval, natural disasters, airline strikes, or illness, Gary Stoller, a travel reporter for *USA Today*, suggests you may need more critical resources such as a travel-assistance company to extradite you and assure your safety. The US State Department is a good reference for specific warnings in countries, and may be of assistance, but the department does not necessarily have the ground resources like specialized companies to comprehensively assist travelers

Carry a list of contact information and services provided by travel-assistance companies that have contracted with your firm. (Ideally, your company monitors countries in which it knows you and your colleagues will be traveling, updates you on brewing issues, and provides assistance in evacuations.) Two well-known companies include International SOS and Frontier Medex—carry their contact information, even if your company doesn't have a contract with them, as well as that of the local US State Department.

CHAPTER 3: **FAMILY AND HOME PREPARATION**

QUICK GUIDE

❖ Anticipate Separation Anxiety
❖ Find a Home Guardian
❖ Provide for emergencies

Separation Anxiety

Family members who express fear when you leave the house or embark on small trips could experience heightened anxiety when you go on longer trips, especially when you are going abroad. Separation anxiety is experienced by adults and children, and differs in "attachment style." Start to address this phobia before you go on your first overseas trip.

Elizabeth Bernstein, a health and wellness reporter for *The Wall Street Journal*, shared in an article some tips for worriers, such as 1) plan special outings for when your loved one is away, 2) recognize when you're overly sensitized, 3) don't ask for reassurance, 4) utilize positive thinking techniques, and 5) keep a journal.

If your family experiences extreme anxiety, it might be helpful to seek professional therapy.

Home Preparation

Unless someone is staying at your home, arrange for your mail to be held at the post office and temporarily stop delivery of newspapers. Enlist a very trustworthy friend, a "home guardian," to check on your home occasionally to ensure the electricity is still on, the structure is intact, the grounds are OK, and the house hasn't been breached.

In addition to providing your home guardian with a set of keys, leave with him or her your insurance policy, names and phone numbers in case of emergencies, and funds, perhaps 200-300 dollars, in case they need to make home repairs. Ask the guardian to keep receipts for insurance or warranty purposes. Provide contact information for an alternate who can watch the house if the guardian has an emergency.

If your house is in an area prone to disasters—hurricanes, earthquakes, or tornadoes—arrange for a service that can put up shutters, shut off gas lines, evacuate animals, and whatever else may be necessary before or after an incident. Your home guardian may have to evacuate or take care of his or her own property in an emergency.

CHAPTER 4: **TRAVEL BASICS**

> **QUICK GUIDE**
>
> ❖ Check, renew, or obtain your passport
> ❖ Join hotel and airline loyalty programs
> ❖ Consider joining an airline club
> ❖ Review your debit and credit card needs
> ❖ Consider obtaining a phone, AAA, or AARP card
> ❖ Obtain business cards
> ❖ Join trusted traveler programs

Passports

New Passports and Passport Card

Almost all the information you'll need for obtaining a passport can be acquired at the website for the US Department of State's Bureau of Consular Affairs (http://travel.state.gov/passport), but use this section as a quick reference. In addition, your local post office provides information on applying for new and replacement passports.

13

If you're traveling by land or sea (not by air) between the United States and Canada, Mexico, Bermuda, or the Caribbean, you can apply for the less expensive US Passport Card. If you're traveling outside North America or internationally by air, you need to obtain a passport.

The procedure for applying for a first-time passport for US citizens requires an in-person visit to a designated post office, clerk of court, public library, or other government office. Find the closest place at the United States Department of State website (http://iafdb.travel.state.gov/) by entering your zip code. Click on the desired facility to see its hours, address, and phone number, appointment requirements, photo availability, and handicap access. You will need to present an application for passport (Form DS-11), proof of US citizenship (birth certificate, Consular Report of Birth Abroad (CRBA), naturalization certificate, or certificate of citizenship), proof of identity (naturalization certificate, valid driver's license, current government or military ID), a photocopy of the ID presented, one passport photo, and appropriate payment. The estimated time for processing applications is less than four weeks, but I suggest applying at least two months in advance.

Expedited Passports

By paying an additional fee and overnight delivery charges at the time of application, you can expedite the processing of your passport. Two-way overnight delivery is suggested. Clearly mark EXPEDITED on the envelope. Monitor the status of your expedited or regular-service application on the Department of State's website.

Expired Passports

Your current passport should be valid at least six months beyond the dates of your trip, and contain at least two blank visa/stamp pages. Adding pages and renewing your passport both take time, so plan accordingly. If your passport is in good condition and you received it within the past fifteen years, you should be able to renew by mail. To do so, download and complete the DS-82 application form, attach to it your most recent passport, include two identical passport photographs and the appropriate fee. You can also expedite this service. For name changes, enclose a certified copy of the legal document specifying the name change. Mail all payments and applicable documentation in a padded envelope to the address indicated on the form. If you are not using overnight delivery service, at least use registered mail so you can track the progress of your package.

TRAVEL BASICS

There is no charge for adding pages to your passport page using routine mail service. You will need to complete a DS-4085 form and mail in your passport as indicated. This may take as long as six to eight weeks, however. Expedited service, which requires a fee and payment for overnight service, takes about three weeks.

If you need your new or renewed passport urgently—in less than two weeks—you should make an appointment at a passport agency. If you have a travel emergency, call the National Passport Center[1] at 1-877-487-2778.

Lost Passports

If you lose your passport while overseas, contact the nearest US Embassy or consulate. An embassy list grouped by region, country and city is at http://www.usembassy.gov. This website also displays embassy hours, travel warnings, visa requirements, and other relevant information about your destination.

If you lose your passport while in the United States, report it and replace it by visiting a passport agency or acceptance facility. You will need to take with you completed forms DS-64 (the statement regarding a lost or stolen passport) and DS-11 (an application for a passport.)

E-Passports

Since August of 2007, the United States has been issuing e-passports with embedded chips that hold data displayed on the photo page of the passport, plus a digital photograph. Passports without chips are valid until the date indicated in the passport.

Hotel and Airline Programs

Join all the airline, hotel, and automobile programs that are free and relevant to your travel, and then accrue points toward free flights or stays when you use their services. These points generally count toward status levels—such as gold, diamond, or platinum—that may result in free upgrades, priority in overbooked situations, and other amenities. Query your coworkers or firm's travel agents to prioritize enrolling in various programs. You can join a hotel or an airline program even before you stay one night at a company's hotels or fly one mile in an airline's planes by phoning them or joining online.

---

1 http://travel.state.gov/passport/npic/agencies/agencies_5150.html

Most airline and hotel websites are closely linked to their parent's name (e.g., Delta.com for Delta Airlines or Marriott.com for Marriot) and are easily found using your favorite Internet search engine. The home page will direct you to where to fill in your personal information and preferences, such as for room and seat location. Download the hotel or airline app to your smartphone to monitor or make changes to your reservations.

The US government requires the name on your airline tickets to match your ID exactly. Whatever name is on your passport should be exactly the same as on your airline accounts. If you've already opened airline accounts and your ID does not match, contact the carrier for instructions.

In the past, I have only used my middle initial on airline accounts, but my passport has my full middle name. My travel agent added my middle name to my tickets and itineraries until I changed my name on my account profiles by sending a copy of my passport and a letter requesting my name change. The airline sent me a new frequent flyer card and lounge card as well.

Airline and hotel sites will assign or ask you to create a log-in name and password or pin number, so that in the future you can make your own reservations online, view your accrued points or mileage, or possibly redeem points and miles for award stays and travel. I am reluctant to write down these log-ins and passwords, out of fear that someone glancing at my diary will then have access to my accounts. This is a legitimate concern considering how often I misplace things. So instead, I write down hints for my passwords, which vary depending on the log-in sites. Most club sites will ask you to create hints, which they can send to you on the occasion you're locked out of their websites after trying to log in too many times. A few suggestions for your passwords and hints:

- Use a combination of numbers, names, and characters (such as exclamation points or questions marks).
- Because it's easy for others to find your mother's, kid's, and pet's names, use names that are less familiar to others, such as that of a former pet, your niece, or your grandmother, but don't indicate this in the hints you write down.
- Change your password frequently and update your hints accordingly.

Frequently, websites will ask if you want to leave a credit card on file. It's not necessary, especially if you're extremely security sensitive, but then you'll have to reenter this information every time you make online reservations.

Airline Clubs

Many airlines have club lounges shared with their key partners, located in airports where they have hubs. The charge to join these clubs can be several hundred dollars a year, although you may receive a discount once you reach an elite status. These lounges are full of comfortable chairs, and offer free water, coffee, and tea, and sometimes snacks and other drinks. Airline clubs are nice oases in busy airports. Other amenities, free or otherwise, may include:

- workstations
- wireless or wired Internet access
- phones
- magazines
- TVs
- printing and faxing
- conference rooms
- alcoholic beverages.

Club membership may grant you access to shorter security lines at some airports.

Confirm with your employer whether you'll be reimbursed for a club membership. If you have elite status with an airline, ask if you can pay for discounted access to that club, and solicit reimbursement for a club with a more expensive fee.

If you travel in first or business class on international trips, you typically will have complimentary access to clubs before your flights. In addition, some credit cards, such as the Platinum American Express, will grant you free access to a limited number of clubs.

Credit/Debit Cards

Credit Cards

You will want at least two credit cards, a primary and a backup in case the first is lost or stolen, or in case the establishment you are patronizing does not take your preferred provider. When traveling to emerging markets, make sure your selected hotels accept credit cards at all. I have stayed at some smaller hotels that required a money order or a cashier's check sent to them ahead of time.

Most credit cards now give you an opportunity to earn hotel, airline, or merchandise points. If you have a favorite airline or hotel, see if they offer branded credit cards with no annual charge.

Credit cards offer different levels of service, typically in ascending order—silver, gold, and platinum—for a yearly fee that can be pretty hefty. For instance, for several hundred dollars, if you are approved, you can order a Platinum American Express that offers you such amenities as:

> upgraded rooms when you check into hotels
> complementary companion tickets on some international airline programs
> shipboard credits when taking cruises
> faster accrual of reward points
> emergency assistance while traveling
> access to professional travel agents

Reward points can then be exchanged for merchandise, travel, and entertainment events. Depending on the frequency you travel or use credit cards, the yearly fee may or may not be worth it.

Before you leave for your trip, make sure you know the spending threshold on your credit cards. Depending on where you're staying, lodging and other expenses can run over five thousand dollars a week.

Debit Cards

Debit cards are particularly helpful when traveling abroad, as you can use them in ATMs to pick up the local currency in many countries at a better rate than in most hotels or airports. You may even be able to make purchases using debit cards in other countries, but Kathy Chu, a reporter for *USA Today*, suggests checking for extra fees attached to using the debit card, or whether you'll forgo (or receive fewer) points and other benefits that come with using a credit card.

You may want to have a separate bank account for the debit card you use while traveling. That way, if your card or card number and pin are lost or stolen, there will only be limited funds accessible. You may need to keep in that account enough money to cover expenses up to a couple hundred dollars per travel day, and for a few extra days.

After paying way too many fees for exchanging currencies in Japan, I discovered that 7 and i's (Japanese version of 7-Eleven) have ATMs that can be utilized by English speakers. There was a fee for the service, but the exchange rate appeared better than that at a hotel. As a result, I picked up some extra yen. This was fortunate because the day I was supposed to fly out, a FedEx plane's accident caused the runway to close, and I was stuck a couple extra days at an airport hotel. Another lesson learned—have access to sufficient cash for a few extra days longer than your expected trip.

Other Cards

Phone Cards

Your cell phone may or may not work in all the countries or cities where you are going, and you may need to use a landline. Dialing internationally can be very expensive and hotel charges can be prohibitive, so check with your personnel or travel office to see if it offers a calling card. The card should have your personal number and pin for you to input when making calls. In addition, you will need country access codes that when dialed, give you access to your carrier to call the United States or other countries. Sometimes these access numbers are provided on small cards to be folded up and placed in your wallet, or you may be able to access them on your provider's website. In some cases, you may use your provider's access codes to charge calls to your personal credit card.

AAA Card

I originally joined AAA for the free roadside service, especially on the many occasions I accidentally locked the keys in my car. The club also offers a fun magazine, assistance in planning trips domestically, discounts at some tourist attractions, and bail bonds service—the latter of which I have not had to use and hope not to.

Recently I discovered while booking a trip online that with some hotel franchises—Hilton and Hyatt, for instance— inputting my AAA number gets me discounted rates at hotels around the world. If you travel frequently, this service might pay for the annual card fee.

AARP Card

I may not necessarily be thrilled that I'm eligible for this card, but it also can be very useful for discounts on hotels, cruises, and other travel-related activities.

Business Cards

Exchanging business cards is a very important part of the introduction process in many countries, especially in Asia. Also, it's quite common that many representatives from management may show up at a meeting, in addition to an interpreter. Therefore, it's wise to order sufficient business cards way in advance of your trip, assuming you will use at least five per meeting. You'll also want to carry extra to exchange with colleagues and new friends.

In Asia, it's not unusual for business cards to be in the local language on one side and in English on the other. You may want to tailor some of your cards to the country you'll be visiting. Check to see if this is permissible in your firm. If your local printer can't do the translation, the hotel to which you're traveling may be able to arrange for some of your cards to contain the local translation.

If you realize you are running short of business cards, you may want to have your office express mail some to you, or you can use a local printer.

I had been in Japan for almost a week. For some of my meetings, I was exchanging six or seven business cards. Before I ran out of cards, my Japanese colleague escorted me to a Kinko's (now FedEx), where my card was duplicated almost exactly.

Trusted Traveler Programs

Global Entry Program

The Global Entry program is a pilot program that allows prescreened members to enter the United States by using automated kiosks located in the arrivals area of some airports that utilize fingerprint biometric technology.

To apply, you must submit electronically an application via the Global Online Enrollment System (GOES) at the US Customs and Border Protection website (www.globalentry.gov). After the application has been reviewed, either your request will be denied, or you'll receive a link to schedule an interview at one of the Global Entry enrollment centers at a participating airport. If you proceed to the interview stage, you will need either a machine-readable US passport or machine-readable permanent resident card, and one other form of identification with your current address. At the interview, your documents will be verified, your eligibility requirements will be finalized, and a digital photograph of your face and your fingerprint biometric information will be taken. If the interview is successful, the Global Entry conditions will be explained, and the automated airport kiosk will be demonstrated.

TSA Precheck-√™

In October of 2011, the TSA initiated a pilot precheck program for select frequent flyers from Alaska Airlines, American Airlines, Delta Air Lines, United Airlines, and US Airways, as well as members of the Customs and Border Protection's Trusted Traveler programs, including Global Entry, SENTRI, and NEXUS. Participating passengers' boarding passes contain a special bar code that, when scanned, may allow them to proceed through less onerous screenings, although they still could be selected for more in-depth screening. This program is expected to expand from the current airports that use it. Monitoring the Transportation Security Administration's website (www.tsa.gov) will provide updates on these various programs.

TOKYO, JAPAN

CHAPTER 5: **TRIP CONSTRUCTION**

> **QUICK GUIDE**
> ❖ Set your most important meetings first
> ❖ Compare overseas fares and determine the duration of your trip
> ❖ Fill in other meetings
> ❖ Plan your intermeeting transportation
> ❖ Consider ways to maximize your travel budget
> ❖ Review your travel documents

Determining the Duration

Traveling internationally is a wonderful but taxing experience, so plan your trip to be comprehensive but well-paced. When first starting to travel abroad, you might want keep your trips to no longer than a week. After you understand your body's rhythms, you can plan longer trips. In general, my colleagues and I have found that overseas trips lasting one to two weeks make the best use of our travel budget, while allowing us to stay on top of our office workload. The exact number of days away will depend on your travel options and business opportunities.

Refining the Focus/Filling in the Schedule

You may have to travel on demand, or you may have the flexibility to design your trips around a goal and within a budget. Plan your trip around the requested travel or your selected theme, specific event, or region, and then fill in blanks in the schedule with opportunistic meetings.

I was a pharmaceutical and UK analyst, and a portfolio manager for accounts which held stocks in companies located all over the world.

At the beginning of the year, I checked the dates international pharmaceutical companies were holding important events, such as Investor Days or R&D symposiums. When I found a cluster of meetings in a region (e.g., Europe or Asia) within a two-week period, I had the nucleus for a trip. (Please see the section regarding traveling around the world if you're feeling more adventurous.)

Once I established the meetings or conferences that were a priority, I blocked out those days for those countries and looked for other regional events of interest. I also reached out to other analysts, heads of other departments, and managers of other offices, and filled my schedule with meetings with current or prospective clients, vendors, or employees.

Using this approach, I set up two to five visits a day in five to eight countries over a two-week period, and made good use of the firm's travel budget.

A schedule like this can be pretty intense and easily derailed. So a couple suggestions:

➢ Determine the dates and locations for your most important meetings.

➢ Look at potential overseas fares around these dates to see what the best arrival and departure days to the region or country are (see more in the maximizing the budget section); your overseas flights will bookend your trip.

➢ Check the holiday schedule for the countries you are planning to visit.

➢ Fill in the other days with meetings of interest to you and your colleagues (see more in the maximizing the budget section).

➢ Travel in a straight line or around the world (more about that in the next section) when possible. For instance, if you're traveling in Europe, you may want to start in the UK, where the time difference is five hours from the US East Coast, and then progress east through France or Germany, then northern and southern Europe, and then finally Eastern Europe. Going in this direction, your body just has to adjust to incremental changes in time zone until you come home. Alternatively, you may want to go to the most distant point, making the biggest adjustment in time first, and then make your way back toward home.

TRIP CONSTRUCTION

- Airports in other countries may be closer to your destination than ones in the same country. Look at a map and see.

- Considering the advance time you need in airports to clear security, and the time it takes to get from airports to city centers, trains are sometimes a better option than planes.

- If there are many meetings a few hours apart, it might be worthwhile to hire a car service.

- Arrange to arrive the night before your most important meetings. You don't want to miss them to due to delays. Do not take the last flight of the day to your next destination. If it's canceled, your entire schedule for the next day will be disrupted.

- Plan to spend successive nights in the same hotel a couple times during your trip. This will give you respite from unpacking and packing and give you a chance to have some laundry done.

- Schedule some downtime—a couple days at a colleague's office, a free day in the weekend, or a couple of evenings that you can look forward to sightseeing or resting. Travel should not be all work. You need and deserve some time to relax.

Maximizing Your Budget

Travel around the World

The ultimate "circle," traveling around the world, is one of the best ways to capitalize on your travel dollars, because airlines often will grant you a discounted pass and allow you, literally, to cover a lot of ground.

My most productive itinerary starts with visiting companies in Japan for four days, which gives me time to travel to Osaka, Kobe, and Tokyo. Potentially I can schedule a side trip to another Asian country. From Asia, I can fly to Europe to visit companies before traveling home.

Although productive, and a great way to rack up some frequent flyer miles, this is a pretty rugged trip. A couple suggestions to enhance your trip and save your sanity:

- Find out from your favorite airline what other carriers you can use to travel on this pass and to accrue award miles. Some of these alternative airlines might have more direct routes than your domestic carriers when going between regions. *For instance, traveling from Europe to South Florida on my main carrier, Delta, usually requires traveling through Atlanta or New York. Two of their European partners are Air France and Air Alitalia, which have direct flights from Miami to Europe and back.*

- ➤ Make sure you know all the rules to use the pass. Normally airlines require that you travel in one direction, make at least three twenty-four-hour stops, spend at least ten nights away, and keep yawns no longer than the shortest leg of your trip. Using a world pass doesn't preclude you from using other airlines for other short trips, which may cost you extra, but make sure you don't violate your pass rules in order to get the best fare.

- ➤ Give yourself at least one day of rest after doing your middle long leg. For instance, try to fly between Europe and Asia on a Friday night or Saturday morning so that you have Sunday to recoup your energy before starting your Monday itinerary.

Travel on Off-Peak Days or Seasons

Many airlines' websites now enable you to search over several days for the best-priced itinerary. The difference in cost between traveling on a heavy travel day and an off day can be thousands of dollars—often worth the cost of an extra night in a hotel.

In international travels, as it is when flying domestically, it's normally cheaper to fly during the week than on weekends. Also, according to Scott McCartney of the *Wall Street Journal*, tickets seem to be less expensive in February.

I received an invitation for a tour of pharmaceutical firms in Japan, and another invitation for a conference in Paris the previous week. My travel budget didn't have room for both trips separately, or for an around-the-world ticket. After checking several airlines' websites and looking at combinations of flights, I bought a round-trip ticket from Miami to Italy, a round-trip ticket from Italy to Paris, and a round-trip ticket to Japan from Italy, and saved approximately three thousand dollars off a round-the-world ticket and set up twenty-five meetings over the two-week period. One caveat: My Tokyo-to-Italy and Italy-to-Miami flights were only about twelve hours apart, and a typhoon heading toward Tokyo almost caused the cancelation of the Tokyo-to-Italy portion. As the ticket to Miami from Italy was nonrefundable, I would have had no recourse but to buy another ticket for home or throw myself on the mercy of Alitalia. So on itineraries as frantic as this one, allow an extra day in between overseas routes to ensure you make your connections.

Compare Airline Fares

On websites for companies such as Travelocity, Expedia, and Priceline, you can input cities and dates of origin and destination, maximum amount of interim stops, and preferred class of service in order to compare costs among some airlines servicing that route. You can then book via those websites, the preferred carrier website (assuming you are using the same airline or partner airlines on the whole trip), or your travel agent. With any of these options, you may also get deals on hotels and rental cars. Many of these travel agencies allow you to download their apps for free to your electronic devices. One caveat: Not all airlines or routes maybe displayed.

According to Dennis Schaal of USA today, by inputting the same information into Routehappy at www.routehappy.com, you can compare amenities (seat pitch, aircraft comfort, Wi-Fi and outlet availability, and flight delays) and flyer satisfaction scores to fine-tune the best flights for you on routes when cost is not your only criteria. You can't make reservations on this site yet, but it will give you choices of other websites where you can complete your travel plans.

Consider Alternate Ports of Entry

Your transcontinental flights will likely be the longest and most expensive part of your trip. Sometimes it's cheaper to fly into and out of a different city, and use a regional carrier or trains to get to your first and last destinations. For instance, while traveling to a conference in Paris, I flew Delta with a special round-trip fare to the UK. Even after connecting on Air France to Paris, my total fare was fifteen hundred dollars less than had I flown back and forth to Paris from Miami.

Travel in Coach

Traveling in coach while overseas can save hundreds of dollars per flight leg, and if the flights are only a couple hours, it may be worthwhile. In days when even peanuts are scarce on US flights, on some carriers such as Air France you might even get a nice sandwich and a split of wine for free.

Travel in Economy Plus

Many airlines provide a class of service in between coach and business class that offers great savings on long trips, with some of the same amenities as business class, such as seats that partially decline, in-seat videos, and better meal and wine lists than what's offered in coach. Amenities differ considerably by airline, route, and equipment, so it's best to check with the airline to see what's offered on your flight. This information may be available on the website.

Travel by Train

While overseas, it might be cheaper and more convenient to travel by train between cities and even countries. Your travel agent should be able to assist you in finding the best alternatives for your travel, but most cities' or countries' websites will offer you information to help you select your best option. A very comprehensive global train guide is sponsored by TrainTraveling.com. This website offers abundant information on routes, fares, and destinations for the major regions around the world. For more information on inter- and intracountry travel, please consult chapter 16: Roaming Abroad.

Book Ahead

Booking many months in advance of a heavy travel season may save thousands of dollars on the fare, but the tickets may come with stiff penalties for changes. *Wall Street Reporter* Scott McCartney suggests that booking two to three months in advance, when airlines are pushing to fill seats, might be better.

Look for Specials

Sign up for e-mail specials with your favorite airline carriers and hotels, and they will e-mail you when there are domestic or international special fares or hotel rates.

While planning a trip to Tokyo, Japan, I went to the Hilton website and discovered a special weekend fare at the Tokyo Conrad Hilton for a junior suite that was not much more expensive than a regular room, and certainly enhanced my stay at the hotel. I also found a special Delta business-class fare to and from Tokyo that required switching planes in JFK, but was almost three thousand dollars cheaper than the fare if I switched planes in Atlanta. The fare required me to stay ten nights in Japan, but I filled my days with more meetings, and it was certainly worth the extra time spent in Tokyo.

Prepay for Travel

Before prepaying for travel, check with your company's travel policy that this is acceptable, and that it will pay for any trip changes made at the company's request.

TRIP CONSTRUCTION

Usually the earlier you book your flights, the cheaper they are. Remember, however, that whenever you decide to ticket them (which typically must be within 24 hours of making reservations in order to keep the fare), your or your firm's credit card will be charged immediately. If you are absolutely sure of your travel dates, you may opt for a nonrefundable fare, which is typically less expensive. Before choosing this option, consider carefully the costs you will incur if you need to make a change, and if there are any refunds if you must cancel the flights. There may be some forgiveness for illnesses, travel interruptions, or family deaths, but generally speaking, you will not receive a refund for canceling international flights unless you pay the higher flexible fare.

Hotels also offer significant discounts if you prepay for your entire stay weeks to months ahead of time. Depending on the hotel policy, if you try to change the reservation, you may be charged for the entire stay. When making this type of reservation, you will be locking in the foreign exchange rate. If the US dollar changes considerably against the currency of your target destination, your stay could become less or more expensive than if you pay at the time of travel. This is another reason for checking your firm's travel policy on prepaying for travel.

Obtaining Travel Documents

Passports

If you're traveling to a foreign country other than Mexico and Canada, you will need a valid passport. If you already have a passport, check to make sure it has not expired, and that you have enough pages to accommodate the stamps for the countries you are visiting. For more information on passports, please refer to chapter 3.

Visas

Some international countries require a visa—a stamp or a page in your passport—that specifies the time period you can stay in the country. Requirements for visas vary by country. You should be able to find what you need online by selecting the Country Specific Information tab at http://travel.state.gov. If you are a US citizen, your visa will be stamped for many countries—such as those in Western Europe, Japan, and South Korea—when you go through their Immigration. For other countries, such as Russia, China, and India, you need to apply for a visa ahead of time. Although you can try to maneuver this process yourself, I would suggest using a visa service such as CIBT[2]. That way, you can track and expedite the progress of your passport through the system.

---

2 us.cibt.com

Obtaining a visa can be expensive and time consuming, so you may want to request a multiple-entry visa for a five-year period, rather than just a single-entry one. Sometimes you can get a visa within days; other times it may take a month. Make sure you have time to get the visas you need so that your passport isn't delayed, and you don't miss your entire trip. If you are cutting it too close, you might want to consider dropping some countries from your itinerary.

ATHENS, GREECE

CHAPTER 6: **PRETRAVEL CHECKUP**

> ### QUICK GUIDE
> ❖ Visit your doctor
> ❖ Get your vaccinations
> ❖ Flying acclimation

Checkups

Traveling can take a toll on your body, and traveling out of the country can even be more taxing. Changes in air pressure, exposure to different climates, and switches in time zones can make a traveler tired, stressed, and more vulnerable to sickness. So even if you've been to a doctor recently, it's time to go back.

To make the most of this appointment, be prepared. Before you show up at your doctor's office, make a list of:

➢ the countries you are going to visit

➢ any medications—over the counter or prescriptions—that you are currently taking

- any severe illnesses that have occurred to you or close family members in the past
- your vaccination history
- a copy of your preliminary itinerary

Armed with this information, your physician might suggest that you take vitamins, aspirin, or sleep aids to ward off discomfort from jet lag or the flu. In addition, you'll want to have written prescriptions for any drugs you may need to fill before or during your trip. Carry the generic names of the prescriptions so you can find alternatives to the brand names while traveling.

My doctor prescribes for me a broad-spectrum antibiotic to carry abroad in case I come in contact with foodborne bacteria or other serious bacterial illnesses. Antibiotics must be taken responsibly to avoid development of resistance. Make sure you use any drugs only when and as prescribed by your doctor.

When traveling overseas, you may be on a flight segment anywhere between six to fifteen hours. Depending on your arrival time, you may want to sleep on the plane. If you find it difficult to do so, talk to your doctor about what medications are safe for you to take. Some sleeping medications may cause adverse effects with alcohol or other prescription drugs.

One of my friends mentioned that, while traveling, she had a bout of food poisoning that was so severe, she could not even keep down an antibiotic. She was saved by taking an Ambien. She was able to sleep and let her body repair so that she could keep down liquids. Now she will not travel without Ambien. Ask your doctor.

Vaccinations

Even in seemingly benign locations, certain viruses, to which US residents are not typically exposed, are endemic. For instance, travelers may come in contact with Hepatitis B in Japan or malaria in India. A visit to the website for the Centers for Disease Control (CDC) or World Health Organization (WHO) will give you an idea of what vaccinations or other preventive measures you need to take for the country or region you are visiting.

Many vaccinations need to be administered months in advance, and some require a series of vaccinations to confer the full benefit of immunity, so arrange an appointment as soon as possible with the appropriate physician. Your family doctor might not stock or be familiar with travel medicine, and you may need to find a clinic or physicians group to ensure you get the right medicine and advice. The latter might be particularly important if you find you will not have sufficient time before traveling to finish the series of shots. In that situation, the doctor might recommend that you take certain precautions, such as using bug spray to avoid malaria-carrying mosquitoes, or drinking bottled water to avoid food and waterborne illnesses. In addition, an experienced physician will be knowledgeable about rashes and side effects for the medicines you will be taking or the shots that are administered.

Flying Acclimation

According to the VALK Foundation, a collaborative venture by the University of Leiden, KLM, and Amsterdam Airport Schiphol, between 20–40 percent of adults in the Western world experience anxiety while traveling by air. There is now a variety of methods to address this fear, including hypnosis, online classes, and even apps. SOAR, Inc. offers DVDs and MP3 downloads that can be purchased at http://www.fearofflying.com/, and a less comprehensive but free app. Other apps of note are Fear of Flying by the VALK Foundation, and Flying Without Fear, offered by Virgin Atlantic.

CHAPTER 7: **TRAVEL WARDROBE, LUGGAGE, AND TOILETRIES**

> ### QUICK GUIDE
> - Check the weather
> - Comb your closet
> - Subscribe to your favorite vendors
> - Assemble some outfits
> - Find practical but stylish shoes
> - Select your luggage
> - Collect and test cosmetics and toiletries

Travel Wardrobe

Reviewing your travel wardrobe months in advance gives you plenty of time to accumulate what you need and what you can fit into one suit carrier. That's right. You should be able to travel around the world with one suit carrier and one computer bag!

Weather Considerations

If you have an idea about where you are going for your next trip, check out the prospective weather using either your iPhone or www.weather.com.

Minimum Essentials

An optimal combination of clothes includes a couple of two-piece suits (each being any combination of a jacket with a dress, skirt, or slacks) and two complementary blouses that can work with any of the outfits. For your downtime, you will want a comfortable set of workout clothes (traveling doesn't give you an excuse to get fat), or a comfortable pair of shorts or slacks, and a polo shirt or cover-up that goes with both your casual and exercise clothes. Finally, you will want a pair of comfortable shoes for exercising or walking.

Color Coordination

Center your travel wardrobe around a color.

I built my wardrobe around black when I first started traveling—a three-piece black suit, another suit with items I could mix and match with black, complementary blouses (a little pink thrown in), and black shoes.

Over time, I discovered that my wardrobe could revolve around any color. After designing mini wardrobes around beige and navy, I evolved into bolder colors, the latest being purple, which, by the way, goes with black.

Value Shopping

Clothes, especially durable ones for traveling, can be expensive if you pay full price. Shoes and accessories are not cheap, either. By planning ahead, you can buy many items at a discount by letting merchants know you want to be notified of their sales.

For instance, many merchants have websites that are divided into slacks, skirts, and suits. The latter is very helpful for those of us who need Garanimals™ to match our clothes. Even better, some merchants such as Ann Taylor and Banana Republic have "collections," which include a variety of clothing, fabrics, and accessories that go together with style. I never would have considered slinky sweaters, faux alligator shoes, fur-trimmed jackets, flared skirts, and tailored shirts in complementary, if not always conservative, colors, but I can wear them now with confidence.

The individual items in suits often cost more than I would spend on an entire year's worth of clothes. By signing up with certain websites, however, I'm notified by e-mail of sales, and sometimes those three-hundred-dollar jackets and two-hundred-dollar skirts can be picked up for a hundred dollars. Outlet malls are also a great place to find your favorite brand names on sale.

Months before you travel, explore different stores on site or online, and keep tabs on those alligator shoes and cashmere sweaters. You may find something to add some spice to your travel wardrobe, and be able to buy them at a discounted price if they go on sale before your trip.

Shoe Selection

You will be dragging, carrying, or kicking luggage possibly for thousands of miles through multiple countries and climates, so one of your most important clothing choices will be your shoes.

I am five foot two on a good day and love the boost wearing stiletto heels give me, but they are not practical for traveling. Heels tilt your posture, carrying luggage puts additional weight on your ankles, and the small little taps amplify the strain on your shoes and your back. Thin heels also have another risk—they get caught in grates and are unstable in snow and on cobblestones. You will look beautiful as you trip and fall, but your feet and ankles will hurt and you will ruin a favorite pair of party shoes.

You don't have to forgo heels entirely, unless your doctor recommends it, but keep the heels thick to support your body and that extra luggage you're carrying, and preferably under two inches.

Henry Ford once said that you could have your car in any color—as long as it's black[3]. Luckily most comfortable yet attractive shoes come in more than one color, but black is not a bad idea for shoes—they will go with a wide variety of outfits. On occasion, my subscription to clothing websites has paid off with shoes that came in dual colors such as navy and white, or black and red that added a touch of style to my travel wardrobe and allowed me to expand my color choices. Red is also a good choice for shoes, because it goes with colors such as gray, black, and navy.

One final tip to find shoes that last longer and look better: consider patent leather. The patina on patent leather withstands the rubbing and crushing your shoes will encounter. If an entirely patent leather shoe seems over the top, a little patent on the toes or on one side offers a nice touch of elegance and a little extra protection.

---

3   www.brainyquote.com

Luggage

When traveling abroad, I carry a computer bag that usually fits under the seat in front of me, and a hanging suit carrier. On occasion, I have used a wheeled computer bag supported by my suit carrier. These two pieces of luggage are usually sufficient for a two-week trip.

Before you choose your luggage, list what you need to carry in addition to your clothes.

When I first started traveling, I had to find room for my clothes, toiletries, a couple of books, and a writing pad; a suit carrier and an attaché were enough. In addition to all of the above, I now carry a notebook computer, a smartphone, an iPod, and chargers and connecting cables for all of the above. Despite these additional electronics, I'm still able to fit enough clothes and accessories into a suit carrier and a computer bag to travel around the world and not have to check luggage.

Garment Bags Versus Rollaboards

You probably will want to use either a rollaboard or suit carrier for your clothes. The former has wheels and comes in many sizes that fit into the overhead bins of most airplanes. Rollaboards facilitate carrying heavy and bulky items through airports and down streets. Still, make sure you can carry your loaded bag up stairways when required.

I usually prefer my suit carrier to a rollaboard, especially in situations when I won't be traveling in business class and overhead space will be at a premium. Suit carriers can be unlatched and stretched over other bags, and even rolled up to fit into tight spaces. Usually a flight attendant can find room for one even on full flights. Also, clothes hung in suit carriers are less wrinkled than when they're folded.

Luggage Color

I have always bought black bags. They are discreet. Too discreet. If everyone has a black bag, it's easy to get them mixed up at a baggage carousel. So you might want to choose a color other than black, but I would not suggest selecting too light a color, or your bag will show the dirt it's bound to accumulate over time.

Computer Bags

If you have to carry a computer and related equipment, then a good computer bag—with enough, but not too many, pockets—is essential. How many pockets? How big a bag? Leather or no leather? What can you afford? All are important questions.

Besides durability, there are two main things to consider when buying a computer bag. Will it fit under the seat in front of you? And can you carry it? Most airlines' websites provide the dimensions under the seats. You want your stuffed computer bag to fit within those dimensions. Many computer bags now come with wheels, which adds convenience but also bulk. If you have to check your computer bag, take out the computer first.

You may be able to order your computer bag online, but heading to your favorite luggage store with all of the equipment you expect to carry is the best way to choose your bag. You can make sure all your cords and phones fit into discreet pockets, that there is room for your PC, books, and/or electronic reader, and that in the end, you can still carry it. Even if you choose a bag with wheels, you will still occasionally need to carry this bag up steps. If you choose a bag without wheels, you will want to ensure you can carry your bag for long distances, such as between Terminals T and E in Atlanta's airport.

Some manufacturers have developed computer bags that allow the computer to be scanned without having to remove it from the case during the security line. The company Tumi labels products that are scan-friendly as T-Pass™. Depending on the airport security team's familiarity with these products, however, you may still have to remove your computer.

Cosmetics/Toiletries

Double-Duty Cosmetics

Purchase and sample your makeup several weeks before your trip in order to avoid allergic reactions. To travel lightly, carry makeup that does double duty. At this time, you are permitted to carry on liquids in containers that are no larger than three ounces, and all of your liquids must fit into one quart-size bag. Therefore, you want to carry as little liquid makeup as necessary. Many mineral-based powder foundations also serve as sunscreens, and some products can be used on lips *and* cheeks.

Sample-Size Makeup and Containers

Luckily, as most cosmetics companies offer sample sizes of their products, you don't have to forgo your favorite brands. Sign up via regular mail or e-mail with your favorite makeup supplier and monitor them for specials or samples.

If you're unable to find your favorite cosmetics in trial sizes, you may be able to transfer liquids and creams into smaller travel-sized bottles that can be bought at wholesale prices at places such as Container & Packing Supply (http://www.containerandpackaging.com). Other than size, consider the material, color, and shape of the containers before making a selection. For instance, a nude or clear color will allow you to monitor product volumes. Plastic containers made of high- or low- density polyethylene (HDPE and LDPE) are better candidates for cosmetics than Polyethylene terephthalate (PET), which is usually for food. An excellent description of characteristics of different materials can be found at the above website.

Cosmetic Brushes

Cosmetic brushes are good tools for applying different types of makeup, but they can get dirty and frayed when traveling. If you require several different types of brushes to fine-tune your appearance, you may want to purchase brush cases specifically made for traveling. One website that I found helpful is Makeup Creations (http://www.makeupcreations.com/p-sets-and-cases.html).

I typically need only one brush, but even so, I like to keep it clean when I travel. So I use a retractable cosmetic brush with a cap that I purchased from Avon's Mark product line.

Other Products

Small, sandwich-sized Ziploc bags are great for carrying small quantities of vitamins or aspirin. Check with your pharmacist or doctor, however, before using these to transport prescription or over-the-counter drugs to avoid potential loss of potency. It's better to carry the original prescription bottle if you'll need to refill the prescription, or if there is some concern with drug interactions. Even for more mundane products such as vitamins, you should mark on the back the generic and brand name of the product, expiration date, and any important notes on administration.

Toothbrush covers that can be bought in bulk at a drugstore allow you to carry a full-sized toothbrush cleanly. Small holes allow for airing out the brush while not letting it dampen other things in your bag. They can be cleaned and reused but also cheap enough to periodically replace.

My aesthetician recommends purchasing an extra product to wear on long flights: a noncomedogenic hydrating cream that can be washed off as soon as you get to your hotel. Vaseline lip balm is helpful in maintaining lip moisture. If you already have a tendency toward chapped lips, you may want to ask your dermatologist for stronger products. Remember to try new products in advance to make sure they don't irritate your skin.

Also, for women, yeast infections aren't necessarily associated with travel, but just in case one surprises you on the road, pack an overnight treatment such as Monistat 1.

LONDON, ENGLAND

CHAPTER 8: **TRAVEL ELECTRONICS**

> **QUICK GUIDE**
>
> ❖ Have a chat with your IT department
> ❖ Review your electronic needs
> ❖ Obtain duplicate power cords
> ❖ Obtain power adaptors
> ❖ Consider benefits/drawbacks of headphones, PDAs, smartphones, and tablets
> ❖ Determine your personal electronic needs
> ❖ Safeguard your devices
> ❖ Download appropriate apps

Business Electronics

IT Advice

Depending on your business needs and personal preferences, there are many electronic devices available for your trip: DVD players, tablets, and iPods for entertainment; and smartphones; computers; and phones for business. Luckily, many of these items can be combined. For instance, you can use your smartphone (in some countries) to make calls, send, and receive e-mail, take photos, and listen to music. But not all of these functions will work everywhere and they eat up battery life. Spend some time with your information technology department or resident electronics expert to ensure:

- you have the electronics you need for the job
- they are compatible with each other and the firm's technology
- they will work or can be activated to work in the countries where you are headed
- you have the necessary cable and adaptor plugs for the countries you'll be visiting

> *My last Blackberry plan allowed me to turn on the phone and data exchange capability (for e-mail) when traveling abroad. The cost for this service was prorated over the time I was abroad. Before one trip, I asked my carrier for an international phone number for its help desk, which I used a landline to call when I could not activate my phone. The help desk walked me through the steps necessary to activate a different provider.*

Before you collaborate with your IT department, check with some local contacts to see what equipment and services they use.

Wireless Cards/Cellular

Acquiring a 3G or 4G card or service for your devices is helpful if you're a heavy user of applications (Microsoft, Excel, PDF) and don't want to limit your access to hotels or pay hotel Wi-Fi rates. I. If 4G or 3G card or chipset is not built into your device, Melanie Pinola of About.com suggests considering the purchase of a 4G or 3G USB modem. Ms. Pinola notes that these modems, also called laptop sticks, are easy to install, can be used on more than one device and may be offer additional functionality, such as portable storage. Some devices have cellular capability to which you can subscribe on a monthly basis. In addition to the cost for the card for 3G or cellular, however, there may be excess charges for roaming and data in foreign countries. There is always a trade-off in cost and convenience.

Adaptors and Cables

Various countries use different magnitudes of power, and the plug on your appliances may not fit in their sockets. Most of the time, you can obtain adaptors from the front desk, business center, housekeeping, or concierge of the hotel where you are staying. For your convenience, order either online or in electronics stores plugs for individual countries, or a travel kit with several adaptors. Not every country requires a different adaptor. For instance, the United Kingdom and Hong Kong use the same outlets. After you get your adaptors, mark them right away, so you don't have to continually recheck which adaptors are for where.

To minimize the number of cords and adapters, carry cables that connect several devices, such as your PDA and iPod, to your computer so they can recharge at the same time. Again, make sure your technology group is comfortable with that arrangement.

I like to carry an old-fashioned Ethernet cable. Wireless service is not necessarily available or reliable everyplace and can be expensive, whereas in some international airports, you can "plug in" for free.

Card Scanners

As a frequent business traveler, you will collect enough businesses cards to quickly fill your desk drawers. Electronic readers can scan business cards and include them in the contact folders of your e-mail system, as well as on your tablet or smartphone.

Personal Electronics

Headphones

Business-class passengers on international flights are usually offered earplugs to help deaden the sound of snoring seatmates, bumping carts, and talking passengers. For us exhausted light sleepers on long flights, that's just not enough. I prefer to wear acoustical or noise-deadening headphones that enhance the music or sound from the movie I am watching, while blocking out most other noises while I'm trying to sleep. Many airlines now lend their international business-class passengers these headphones, but you should check with your carrier to see on what routes they are available.

Not all headphones are the same. I strongly suggest you check them out in person before buying them. Some considerations:

> ➤ Price and bulkiness. The cheaper versions seem less bulky but may not offer the same quality.

- ➢ "On the ear" or "around the ear" depicts whether the earpiece rests on the lobe or encompasses it. Depending on individual tastes, these offer different aspects of comfort and sound quality.

- ➢ Acoustical or sound-deadening. Both types enhance sound, although the latter seem better in blocking out noise. There is a trade-off in bulk and battery use.

Electronic Books

Typically I carry three or more books to read while traveling. I leave behind what I finish, and sometimes I buy more at English sections of bookstores that can be found at train stations and airports.

Electronic books are an alternative means of carrying around reading material. Amazon provided one of the earliest electronic readers called the Kindle, with which you can sample, purchase, and download a book in less than a minute, from a library of over a million titles to a device that weighs less than a paperback. You also can access newspapers and magazines for a monthly charge. The latest generation Kindle Paperwhite is lighter, and according to the manufacturer, has no screen glare in bright sunlight and longer battery life. Sony, Barnes and Noble, Apple and Kobo also offer electronic readers, some embedded in other devices, with varying capabilities and sold at different price points. It's worthwhile comparing the various features of these products, and even determining if you can download a reading app to one of your current devices, before investing in an E-Book reader.

Personal Digital Assistants

Personal Digital Assistants (PDAs) are basically pocket-sized computers that are good for business travelers involved in niche businesses, who need to interact with their companies' databases to track shipments, update data, access information, and maintain contact lists. For the most part, smartphones are taking over this market, although PDAs may be more appropriate for heavy document and spreadsheet users who can't carry a laptop.

According to *Consumer Search*, items you should consider when purchasing a PDA include:

- ➢ Memory. The more applications you want to run, the more total memory you will need.

- ➢ Functions. Similar to a smartphone, you can have additional functionality on PDAs, such as a video player, camera, or GPS navigator. It might be worth investing the extra funds in a model that allows you to do without something else you would normally carry.

- Internet access. You may achieve this through Wi-Fi or Bluetooth, depending on your location and other equipment you're using.
- Support. What will your in-house technology group support? If this is a business PDA, you want to make sure the functionality is compliant with the technology in your office.

Smartphones

Smartphones are typically a combination of devices such as: a phone with international capabilities, a music player, and an Internet device that permits access to e-mail and web browsing. Several companies, including Blackberry, Apple, and Google, offer smartphones. As mentioned in a previous chapter, these phones can download many free or low-cost apps that can greatly enhance your travels.

In addition to checking what type of device your firms will reimburse and support, Daniel Dumas of *Wired* magazine recommends considering:

- cost of phone, cost of plan, mandatory contract length, and any other fees
- battery life
- screen functionality
- keyboard access
- camera resolution
- voice response
- weight
- number of applications, and ability to multitask

Other considerations for choosing and using smartphones include:

- Assuming accessing your e-mail is important, check to make sure your enterprise e-mail and network security system supports use of the selected smartphone.

- Review the international capability of your smartphone carrier to make sure it will be operable in the countries where you are going.

- Download applications before you travel abroad, as the network might not be accessible overseas, or there maybe additional data charges while roaming.

- Make sure your smartphone is activated for international travel before you leave the United States.

- According to AT&T, you can minimize international charges by buying an international data package, turning data roaming off until you need to access the data, using Wi-Fi instead of 3G/GRPS/Edge, turning off Fetch New Data, and checking e-mail and sync contacts and calendars manually.

I have been traveling to Paris for two decades. I always have to pick up a new map of the train system and city map when I arrive, and I listen to French CDs months in advance in order to refresh my language skills.

The year I gave my husband an iPhone as a gift, we vacationed in France, his first time. Within hours after the tickets were purchased, my husband downloaded applications for Metro Paris, which helps you plot your way through Paris; Coolgorilla French, which provides phrases in French for all the basic activities (and says them out loud); PARIS software, full of general information about Paris; Drink Pro, whose purpose you can probably guess; and a bunch of games that kept him occupied on the flights. I was a bit jealous.

Netbooks, iPads, Touch-Screen Tablets

There is a whole new array of portable, multifunctional devices that combine Internet connectivity, office software, e-mail, downloadable applications, e-book readers, and keyboards. These new products in turn create a series of upgrade cycles that will constantly tempt you to buy the next new product (or put it in on your wish list) and squish it into your carry-on bag.

Stop! Ask yourself if what you want to buy will really add value to your travel. Consider the following before opening your wallet:

- A new product should significantly add to your productivity or comfort while traveling, or enable you to downsize the amount of electronics and cords you have to carry.

- Your IT department may be able to steer you toward the most efficient, cost-effective compatible products, or recommend you wait until a new product is available.

TRAVEL ELECTRONICS

> Get a loaner and try it out before buying. If this isn't possible, find a friend or colleague who has used the product and can give you the pros and cons.

> Look in your carry-on and at your budget. Is it worth it?

Curling Irons

For a minimalist traveler like me, this seems like an odd selection, but a curling iron is useful to spruce up my hair on mornings when there is not enough time to shampoo. There are portable curling irons, such as X5 Superlite, that are light, foldable to minimize space, and come with special pouches that prevent the cooling iron from burning your clothes.

Hairdryers

Except for one hotel in Hungary (where I requested one from housekeeping), and in Las Vegas (where I had to wait an hour for one), I always have found a hairdryer in the hotel room. You can purchase portable ones from most major personal appliance vendors.

Safeguarding

According to Rolfe Winkler, a reporter covering technology for *The Wall Street Journal*, theft of electronic devices is growing exponentially due to the thriving second-hand market. Sometimes the criminals are violent, with a backup thief "taking out" the victim who gives chase.

Public Use

Avoid using the devices in public, especially on public transportation, where a thief can steal and run away quickly.

Engraving

Engraving your electronic advice is not only stylistic, but, according to *USA Today's* Scott McCartney, also can help you reclaim your device or assist others in finding it in case it's misplaced. You may want to use a first initial and a work address or phone number if you don't want to be contacted on your cell phones or at home. You can also label devices with a business card if engraving isn't possible, or enable ID information to appear on the screen even if the device is locked.

Highlighting

Purchase a uniquely patterned or colored case for your electronics so they are easier to spot or identify if misplaced.

Register

Register your device with the manufacturer, and keep a record of serial numbers in case you lose the device or need documentation for insurance.

Store Data

Enable Cloud or other secure data storage for electronics on which you have sensitive programs or files.

Enable Tracking Programs

Turn on functions, such as Find My iPad, that allow you to find your device if you are separated from them.

Helpful Apps

In addition to the apps that are mentioned elsewhere, I have found the following to be useful:

- ➤ FlightTrack allows you to monitor the progress of flights. This is especially helpful for someone else monitoring your flights, or for you to monitor the plane that will be taking you on your flight. Sometimes there are plane changes, so confirm with the airline the status of your outgoing flight.

- ➤ FlightBoard lets you view the arrival and departure boards at the airport. Similar to FlightTrack, it's useful for anyone monitoring your flight or the incoming plane for your next flight.

- ➤ FaceTime, which you can use to check in with your loved ones at home.

TRAVEL ELECTRONICS

- Wi-Fi Finder, the best way to locate the nearest Wi-Fi paid or free hotspots.
- TripAdvisor lets me read what others have to say about restaurants and attractions near the area I'll be visiting, and I can also share my opinions.
- Fly Delta, Hilton, and any other airline and hotel app that helps you monitor or change your reservations while traveling.
- Tube Deluxe, Paris Metro, Metro Athens, and other public transportation apps.
- Spanish, French, and German Coolgorilla apps that categorize words in local languages.
- With iSpeak, I say what I want to say, press a button, and voila—a voice repeats the phrase in the local language.
- Ultralingua is a very detailed app that provides translation of phrases, words, and numbers, and even provides verb conjugations.
- World Clock is a very helpful app when you are traveling through multiple time zones.
- Game apps such as Blackjack, Sudoku, and Whirly Word can help you pass the time.
- HBO GO, which requires a subscription to HBO and your local cable company.

SEOUL, SOUTH KOREA

CHAPTER 9: **FOREIGN LANGUAGES AND CULTURES**

> **QUICK GUIDE**
> ❖ Select a language course
> ❖ Review social and business norms

Now that you know to where you're going, learn a few words or increase your proficiency in the language of your destination. Words and phrases such as "excuse me," "please," "thank you," and "my name is…" are easy to learn, and will win you a lot of goodwill from your foreign hosts. It also helps to be able to count in the local language, especially while you are buying merchandise in stores, and when you're waiting for flights to be announced.

From the airport in Paris, I took a train to the Gare du Nord station, where I intended to take a taxi to my next destination. I entered the cab with "Bonjour. Excuse-moi, je parle que peu français, mais je dois allez a Hotel Hilton Arc de Triomphe." On the way to the hotel, the cab driver complimented me on my little French, and then went into a tirade in French over Americans' inability to speak any other languages besides English, and berated me for not taking the Metro to my final destination. At least my basic skills

51

got me a lift. After he dropped me off, two English gentlemen asked through the window, "Could you take us to...?" The cab driver ignored them and drove off into the sunset, leaving the two chaps bewilderedly looking around for another ride.

Self-Taught Language Courses

There are myriad approaches to learning a new language, if I had infinite time and money, I would attend a class or find a tutor. I have neither of the above, but I do spend hours in the car, so alternating between language and music CDs has worked well for me. I have tried several different courses, each with different advantages.

Foreign Language Institute

This comprehensive, in-depth course delves into vocabulary and grammar. I also found it to be the best value for my money. I recently switched over to the French CDs from cassettes, and was a little disappointed in the sound quality and the elimination of the translation sections, where at least some of the lessons were in English. I recently bought the MP3 Turkish course that came with a PDF manual. It's very detailed, but you will need to augment your listening with some periodic references to the book—not a good idea while driving unless you have to sit for a long time at traffic lights. But if you have some time on your lunch hour, or on a bus, train, or plane, this would be my recommended approach.

Pimsleur Approach

Learning Italian with this approach was fun. You barely need to reference a book, and you will be introduced slowly to vocabulary and grammar. There is plenty of repetition, with the drawback being it's slow going. You are going to cover less per CD than the Foreign Language Institute methodology, so covering the same amount of material is more expensive but fun.

Learn in Your Car

With the Learn in Your Car Series, the speaker says the word in English and then in the foreign language. It is a tedious but effective way of reviewing vocabulary, and learning some phrases and numbers in a foreign language.

FOREIGN LANGUAGES AND CULTURES

In-Flight

I downloaded the In-Flight Korean Living Language Course to my iPod. If I had not already reviewed level one of the first Foreign Language Institute version, I would have been lost. The lessons, however, are fairly inexpensive.

Culture

Before traveling to new countries, it is worthwhile to review some of the local customs. A quick check of your neighborhood or online bookstore should give you plenty of options, with titles such as *Culture Smart* or *Culture Shock*, for even the most unusual places, such as Egypt. Of course, the unusual places are where you need the most guidance.

Some general practices when traveling and doing business abroad:

- The volume of your voice should be the same of those around you. Shouting will not make you better understood.
- Be polite and patient. You will more likely accomplish your goals that way.
- Most international businesses have not embraced business casual, so dress professionally and keep clothes in good repair.

The next couple of sections give some advice on country-specific cultural items, courtesy of the International Business Center, except where otherwise noted.

China

Business Cards. Present and receive cards with both hands. Never write on a business card or put it in your wallet or pocket. Use a card case.

Business Attire. Both women and men should dress conservatively for business functions and in casual settings. Jeans are not appropriate for business meetings. Colors should be subtle and neutral. Women should avoid revealing clothing, high heels, and short-sleeved blouses.

Business Meetings. Appointments must be set up, and being on time is critical. Bowing is the most common way to greet, but you may shake hands if your Chinese counterpart offers his. Use formal titles, but the Chinese may use a Western nickname. The most important member of your company or group should lead your part of the meeting. The business process may be slow, and the Chinese may wait for an auspicious day to make a decision. Be patient. Allow the Chinese to leave the meeting first.

<u>Social Customs.</u> Do not use large hand movements, point when speaking, use your index finger to point (use an open palm instead), or put your hand in your mouth. Personal contact is avoided; a man generally will not touch a woman in public. Arrive on time or early; do not discuss business at meals; and do not eat or drink prior to the host doing so. You should taste all of the dishes, but do not eat all of your meal or the host will assume you are still hungry. Do not drop the chopsticks (this is bad luck) or place them upright in your bowl (they look like joss sticks and connote death). Women do not usually drink at meals. Tipping, in the past, was considered insulting, but the practice is becoming more common.

Japan

Source: Venture Japan: www.venturejapan.com

<u>Business Cards</u>. Carry at least a hundred for a one-week business trip, preferably double-sided, with English on one side and Japanese on the other. Always present the business card with two hands and a small bow, starting with the most senior official. Accept the card with both hands and say thank you: *arigato gozaimasu*. Never write on or fidget with the cards, store them carefully, and never forget them.

<u>Business Attire</u>. Professional women need to distinguish themselves from the "office ladies" who typically wear company-specified uniforms. This is a fashion-conscious society, and professional women frequently wear designer clothes at least to and from work, following the same seasonal color patterns as men. For work, they generally don't wear high heels, short skirts, or jewelry, and they tie back long hair. Those of us visiting Japan may not be expected to dress exactly this way, but dressing tastefully will likely gain you respect.

Men usually wear dark suits in the winter and gray suits in the summer, with a white shirt (half sleeves in the summer). Avoid black suits, white shirts, and black ties—an outfit associated with funerals.

Business Meetings. Confirm your meetings a few hours ahead of time; arrive at least ten minutes in advance; and call ahead at least one hour, if possible, if you are going to be late. Wait to be directed as to where to sit, as this is arranged according to custom. Plan or provide an agenda—you may be requested to submit questions ahead of time—and try to keep the meeting time within the planned length. Take lots of notes, and expect that they will, too, and hold you to any promises made.

Social Customs. Do not blow your nose in public. Do not shake hands unless that appears to be the norm. Do not ask personal questions, make derogatory remarks, or pat anyone on the shoulder. Using mobile phones to make phone calls in public transportation or during meetings is literally frowned upon. Mobile phones may be used for reading, or sending/receiving messages or e-mails in appropriate public areas.

India

Business Attire. Women should wear conservative dresses or pantsuits, and avoid using leather products, as Hindus revere cows.

Business Meetings. Business may be conducted over lunch, but be sensitive to the fact Hindus do not eat beef and Muslims do not eat pork. Use professional titles when addressing Indian executives.

Social Customs. Never touch someone's head, whistle, wink, point your feet at a person, or wag your finger. Standing with your hands on your hips is considered an angry or aggressive posture. Women should keep their upper arms, chest, back, and legs covered, and should wear long pants when exercising.

Russia

Business Cards. Carry plenty of business cards, with one side printed in English and the other in Russian.

Business Attire. Women should dress conservatively. Avoid flashy or gaudy outfits.

Business Meetings. Be on time for business meetings, but do not be surprised if your colleague is not prompt. Russians can be very patient, and you should be, too, if you really want to achieve your goal.

Social Customs. When shaking hands, make sure you take off your gloves. At formal events, check coats and other objects at the front door of the establishment. Do not show the soles of your feet and do not prop them on furniture. Having a drink or toasting is part of the ritual, and it is rude to refuse. Avoid speaking or laughing too loudly.

Saudi Arabia

Source: The Saudi Network: www.the-saudi.net

Business Cards. Cards should be printed in English on one side and Arabic on the other.

Business Attire. Conservative business suits are recommended. Women should wear long skirts, elbow-length or longer sleeves, and unrevealing necklines.

Business Meetings. Although informing hosts about your intent to meet with them is important, it's better to pin down an exact time for the meeting after you have arrived in the country. When setting your travel plans or requesting a meeting, take into consideration the religious holidays of Ramadan and hajj and daily prayer breaks. Expect that there may be many meetings before business is discussed, and that they'll be long as both sides become comfortable with each other. Initial meetings may be leisurely, with interruptions by phone calls or visitors. At the beginning of the meeting, each person is expected to be greeted with an individual handshake while standing, although Saudi men may be reluctant to shake a woman's hand. The Saudi executives may not take notes during the meeting, and may rely more heavily on memory.

Social Customs. Typically, foreign executives will be served first. Invitations for meal and coffee are usually paid for by the inviter. During Ramadan, it may be best to refrain from eating or drinking when in the company of someone observing the fast. Saudis may stand close to men during conversation, and may use body contact to emphasize a point. It is important to not draw back. Except for Muslim men experienced with Western culture, it's unusual for them to shake hands with a woman or engage in conversational body contact. The right hand is used for all public functions, but talking with one's hands or gesticulating is considered inappropriate. One should not ask about wife or daughters but may ask about family or children. There may be gender separation in public places such as hotels or restaurants.

France

<u>Business Attire</u>. Women should dress conservatively in well-tailored clothing, without bright or gaudy colors or glitzy objects.

<u>Business Meetings</u>. Set up meetings in advance. I have read that punctuality is treated casually in France, perhaps for social engagements, but I would recommend striving to be on time for business meetings, and calling ahead if there is a delay. Shake hands when arriving and departing. Handshakes will likely be brief. Always knock before entering a room, and respect people's need for privacy.

<u>Social Customs</u>. Converse rather than lecture. Maintain a voice level comparable to your hosts. Avoid being too loud.

Germany

<u>Business Attire</u>. Normally very conservative, such as dark suits and white blouses.

<u>Business Meetings</u>. Punctuality is very important. Shake hands at the beginning and end of the meeting, and reciprocate with a bow if that is offered. Men, when introduced to women, may wait until she extends her hand before extending theirs. Avoid distracting humor. Age takes precedence over youth; the eldest person will enter first in a group meeting.

<u>Social Customs</u>. Allow for more individual personal space than you would in the United States. Chewing gum is not appropriate during conversation. Even if you've known someone for a long time, you may still shake hands when meeting again.

Italy

<u>Business Attire</u>. Good clothes and fashion are extremely important in Italy. Women should dress in quiet, expensive elegance.

<u>Business Cards</u>. Italians may carry two types of business cards for business and personal information.

Business Meetings. Be punctual for meetings, but don't be anxious if your host is a little late. At a business function, the most senior or eldest person present should be given special treatment. Both sexes use handshakes. It is not uncommon for several people to speak at the same time at business functions. Italian executives may use cell phones during meetings.

Social Customs. Avoid talking about religion, politics, and World War II, or asking someone you just met about the person's profession. Good topics are Italian culture, art, food, wine, and family films.

Spain

Business Attire. Dress is more formal than that in other European countries, but good taste is appreciated. Avoid flashy colors.

Business Cards. Cards should be two-sided, with one side in English and the other in Spanish. Present the Spanish side to your Spanish colleague.

Business Meetings. Be punctual, but flexible with your expectations for others. Relationships are very important in Spain, and meetings may be used to build rapport before sorting out business. Meetings may take longer than expected. Most executives speak English, but it's wise to have your business materials in Spanish as well. Spanish executives may leave their cell phones on and take calls during meetings. Don't be surprised if business is conducted over lunches and dinners.

Social Customs. Avoid wearing shorts in public. Men who are close may exchange a hug, and women may exchange a small hug and kiss on each cheek.

United Kingdom

Business Attire. Women have more flexibility in their choice of colors and styles, but they are still expected to wear relatively conservative clothes.

Business Meetings. Always be punctual or a few minutes early. Decision-making should not be rushed. Don't expect to maintain eye contact. Avoid staring or asking personal questions.

Social Customs. Handshakes are a typical way of greeting between men and women, but other than that, touching another person is not appropriate. Personal space should be respected. It is not typical to carry on cell phone conversations while you're having business meetings. Avoid loud talking and disruptive behavior.

Argentina

Business Attire. Dress is extremely important and conservative. For women, white blouses and dark suits are typical. Native (Indian costume) is not appropriate.

Business Meetings. Prior appointments are necessary; reconfirm the meetings one week in advance. Don't be surprised if they are in the evening. Be punctual, but be prepared to wait thirty minutes if you are meeting with someone important. The meetings may run long and past their allotted time. There may be several minutes of small talk before the meeting starts, and there may be several meetings necessary before trust is established. Guests are escorted to their chairs; the visiting senior executive will be placed opposite the Argentine senior executive. During the meetings, take a relaxed approach, maintain eye contact, and minimize gestures.

Brazil

Business Attire. Three-piece suits distinguish executives from office workers. Women should wear conservative attire and have manicured nails. Avoid wearing the combination of yellow and green, which are the colors of the Brazilian flag.

Business Meetings. Make appointments two weeks in advance; do not try to drop by without an appointment. Especially in San Paulo and Rio, business meetings are expected to start on time. Business meetings usually start with casual talk; let the host initiate the conversation. Handshaking for a long time is common, both at the beginning and end of a meeting. Make sure you shake everyone's hand before leaving.

Social Customs. Do not use the OK signal, which is considered rude. Pinching the earlobe between the thumb and finger is a sign of appreciation. Avoid discussing Argentina, politics, poverty, religion, and the rain forest. Good topics are soccer, family, and children.

Venezuela

<u>Business Attire</u>. Dress for men is conservative. Fashion is important to women, so they should wear their best business clothes and pack a cocktail dress.

<u>Business Cards.</u> Cards should be printed in English on one side and Spanish on the other, and should be presented immediately after introduction.

<u>Business Meetings</u>. The meetings are punctual and small talk is minimal. Morning meetings may be followed up with a luncheon invitation. Two senior executives should sit facing each other. Posture is important so avoid slouching. Avoid dominating the conversation.

<u>Social Customs</u>. Businesswomen going out alone with businessmen may be misconstrued. Venezuelans tend to stand close to each other when conversing, and Venezuelans may touch each other's arms or jackets during conversation. Handshaking is common with both sexes; good friends may hug and women may kiss cheeks. Avoid discussion of local unrest, inflation, and politics, but business, art, history, and literature are good topics.

South Africa

<u>Business Attire</u>. Dress well. Western dress is acceptable, but African women may wear a sari.

<u>Business Cards</u>. There is no formal exchange protocol.

<u>Business Meetings. M</u>ay be over lunch or dinner, but appointments should be made starting at nine o'clock in the morning. Do not rush the meeting or discussions.

<u>Social Customs</u>. Handshakes are common, but the type of handshake may vary. Use titles and surnames to address people.

EPHESUS

CHAPTER 10: **ITINERARY CREATION**

> **QUICK GUIDE**
> ❖ Plot your itinerary
> ❖ Map your itinerary
> ❖ Review your seat selection

Plotting Your Itinerary

By the week before you leave, you should have your tickets for your trains and planes, and the times and locations of your meetings. Now make sure they all fit together. Create a table for each day of your trip. In the first column, list each hour. In the next column, start each day with the hotel in which you will awake (or the overnight flight you are taking), and include every meeting, venue, and mode of transportation for every hour of the day. In the third column, next to each entry, put in the details: names, addresses, and phone numbers for hotels; carriers; flight numbers; cities of departure; airports; departure and arrival terminals; dates and times of arrival and departure; class of service and seat, if available; names of carriers and drivers for car services; times and locations of pickups and drop-offs; and estimated time of arrival at each destination. Entitle the final column, and reconfirm everything.

Going into this much detail might seem excessive, until on one of your trips you find that the driver expected to take you to the most important meeting showed up in the wrong city, at the wrong hotel, on the wrong day. Or you show up at Tegel airport in Berlin, whereas your flight actually leaves from Berlin's Tempelhof airport, or your hotel reservation is canceled because your overnight flight arrived on June 6 and your reservation was for June 5. All of these things have happened to me.

Once you have finished your itinerary, review it one more time. Check each date, flight, hotel reservation, and confirmation number with the confirmation or itinerary from each hotel, travel agency, airline, or provider of ground transportation. If possible, reprint the confirmation slip from the hotels or airlines to make sure there have been no changes, and then check the appropriate reconfirm field. For every meeting, reconfirm by phone or e-mail the meeting date, location, participants, and contact name. At the same time, offer your contact information and that of your assistant or office point person, so that any changes that occur can be relayed while you are traveling. Also, this is a great opportunity to ask the company contacts to direct you to a website that has directions to their locations, or to request that they email or fax you directions in both the local language and English. Check off in the last column of your itinerary sheet every meeting that is reconfirmed.

Make three copies of your itinerary—one for yourself, one for your office contact, and one for your family or home contact—and save each in a folder or binder marked with your name, travel dates, and the major regions covered by the trip. Distribute them accordingly. The itinerary should also be saved electronically to whatever device will be carried on the trip, and also provided in this form to your assistant and family.

Mapping Your Itinerary

After mapping your itinerary, start another folder with directions, and preferably maps, to each destination. This is also another chance to make sure the logistics of the trip match the anticipated meetings.

If you don't know how to get to the airport, you can retrieve a map from MapQuest, Google Map, or the airline's or airport's website. Note carefully the commute time, and allow 50 percent extra in case of accidents, construction, or other delays. For international trips, you will want to arrive at the airport at least two hours ahead of time in case security lines are long. I suggest arriving three hours ahead of the flight. If you are fortunate to clear ticketing and security with extra time, you can rest in the lounge or go shopping.

For every segment of your trip, document each step of the journey. For instance, when your flight arrives at the airport, how are you getting to your hotel or first meeting after you go through Customs and Immigration? Will there be a driver waiting for you? Where will he be waiting? Outside Customs with a sign with your name, or at the curb outside the airport? Will you be taking a taxi? Are those located on site? If so, where? Will you be taking a train or a bus? Where do you catch the train? Where do you buy tickets? Where does it drop you off and how do you get from there to the hotel? Or does the hotel have a shuttle service? If so, where's the pickup point? Map every step possible from stop to stop.

If you are taking a cab or a car, don't assume your driver knows exactly where you are heading. Pull directions, in the local language and English, from the hotels' or companies' websites, as well as a close-up map surrounding your destinations.

Does this seem too extreme? In my first visit to Japan, I had faxed to me a map—but not directions—for the office of my first destination. As I waited in line for a taxi, I explained to the very polite bellman, who spoke very good English, where I had to go. He then nicely explained it to the friendly cab driver. The driver expeditiously drove me to the office building, where I alighted twenty minutes early for my first meeting.

But it was the wrong office building, the kind information officer told me, when I couldn't find the investment banking firm's name. He pointed to a very large hill and told me my destination was on the other side. There was no way I was going to make it over that hill and in time for my meeting. My first meeting in Japan and I was going to be late. So I did what I had to do.

I stepped into the street and flagged down the first cab I saw. The driver must have been in shock to see a five-foot-two blonde in the middle of Tokyo, so he stopped. I got in the cab and smiled and pointed at the map. The driver took the map from my hand, nodded, put the taxi in drive, took off over the hill, and dropped me off at the correct office building. I tipped him ridiculously. He drove off laughing. I am glad I had that map.

Collect all your directions and maps in chronological order, and store in a folder to put in your carry-on. Make copies for your office and your family, and save electronically as much as possible.

Selecting Airplane Seats

If you did not receive a seat assignment when you ticketed your flight, or if you want to confirm your seat assignment in case there was an equipment change, here is another chance to choose the best seat for you.

Selecting a Seatmate

According to Nancy Trejos of *USA Today*, social websites such as Planely.com and Satisfly.com will help you choose your seatmate on some flights. To use Satisfly, register at the website or find it on Facebook, indicate your mood (business or casual chat, work or relax), set up a desired neighbor profile, and you will be provided with a seatmate. This option is also available at certain carriers such as KLM and Malaysian Airlines.

Selecting the Zone

This applies both to domestic routes and when you are flying on coach or express flights.

Although this will vary by carrier, many airlines will board flights by zones that will be printed on the boarding card, or they will call out rows when boarding. Business class and elite-status passengers board early in the process. Airlines then usually board the rest of the passengers from the rear of the plane forward.

By boarding early, you have a higher likelihood of finding room for your carry-on luggage. Furthermore, the closer to the boarding door you sit, the quicker your chance to exit the plane, which is important when connections are tight.

Selecting the Level

Many international flights offer seats on the upper level, which is accessible by stairs. This area of the plane for me is quieter and more conducive to rest. The drawback: carrying your luggage up and down the stairs upon embarking and disembarking.

Selecting the Row

Bulkhead rows have partitions in front of them rather than another row of seats. Bulkhead seats normally offer a little more space between your feet and the wall, and the absence of passengers in front of you who might lean back into your personal space.

On the other hand, depending on the aircraft, entertainment systems and tray tables may be on the wall rather than on the seat in front of you or in your armrest, and might be more difficult to reach or see. In addition, you don't have a seat in front of you with space underneath for you to store your personal item, which is then accessible during the flight. If you are running late, this space might save you from having to gate-check an item.

Some rows on the plane are designated exit rows. Since these are the rows through which people will exit in an emergency, they are usually more spacious and offer more legroom. Whoever sits in an exit row, however, takes on the responsibility of assisting during an emergency evacuation. There are certain restrictions on passengers on US carriers who choose to sit there, such as:

- ➤ You must be able to understand and speak English well. This may be different in some countries, but for the most part, English is the global language for aviation.
- ➤ Age. Would you want your fifteen-year-old directing other passengers in the event of an emergency?
- ➤ You can't be accompanied by an animal in the cabin of the plane. *Save the person in the seat next to me or my cute little poodle? I'm saving the poodle.*
- ➤ Willingness and ability to assist the cabin crew in the event of an emergency, which usually means that you are not disabled, you can lift and jettison the exit door (which is forty to sixty pounds), and that will you stay calm in emergencies and follow the directions of the crew. The crew will confirm that you are qualified to sit in the exit row. If you cannot or are unwilling to assist in an emergency, offer to sit someplace else. There will be plenty volunteers to switch with you.

Selecting the Seat

Do you want to curl up by the window or sit on the aisle so you don't have to crawl over several people to use the bathroom? Or do you feel really lucky and think a middle seat could place you between two men of your dreams? Of course, you could end up between two gigantic people who fall asleep on you.

Confirming and Changing Seats

If your preferred seat isn't available when you make your reservation, periodically pull it up online and move to your preferred seat if it becomes available. Numbers indicate the row to which you will be assigned. Letters indicate window, aisle, or middle seats.

Airlines typically hold preferred seats for their elite passengers up until the day of the flight, so don't give up. When you check in either online, at a kiosk, or at a counter, see if your favorite seat has opened up.

BARCELONA, SPAIN

CHAPTER 11: **PREWEEK PREPARATIONS**

QUICK GUIDE

- ❖ Assess the weather
- ❖ Review your clothing selection
- ❖ Take inventory of medicine and toiletry
- ❖ Forward or electronically save important documents
- ❖ Copy passport and wallet contents
- ❖ Back up your hard drive

Assess the Weather

Before you select your travel clothes, check the weather at your destination to make sure you have all the proper gear, especially outerwear. Your electronic itinerary might have links that will direct you to a website for the weather in your destination, or you can monitor the The Weather Channel at http://www.weather.com. Hotel pages and the home pages of cities where you'll be traveling might also have weather information.

Select the Proper Clothes

Now that you know the expected weather at your destinations, check your wardrobe one more time to make sure you have the proper clothes and accessories (e.g., gloves, hats, and boots) and that they are in good repair. You have a whole week to fix the heel of your shoes, dry clean your suit, or buy that pair of gloves.

One conundrum on round-the-world trips is packing for wide variations in weather while still not carrying too many clothes. A light wool blazer that can go over a simple dress or with a shirt and slacks is very helpful in these situations. You should not have to pack it; wear it on board with a dress or casual clothes, and use it for protection against overly air-conditioned planes. If you are traveling in business or first class, you can hand it off to the flight attendant for safekeeping. In that case, make sure you stow valuables in one of your carry-ons.

Obtain Medicines and Toiletries

Inventory your medicines, and make sure you have enough for the duration of the trip, plus a few extra days in case you are delayed.

The toiletry checklist at SmartPacking.com should be helpful when you want to gather toiletries or OTC medicines that you might need on your trip. Most of these items can be bought while you are traveling, but that might not be an option if you are pressed for time, plus foreign packaging can be difficult to read. If you are not checking bags, limit your liquids to three ounces or less. There is flexibility when it comes to personal medicines, but when possible, carry travel sizes available at your local pharmacy, grocery stores, or other cosmetics provider.

Make sure you check the expiration date on items you already own. If anything is past the expiration date, purchased longer than six months ago, or if you can't remember when you bought it, dump and replace.

Forward Documents

When possible, store and forward presentations and business documents electronically. When hard copies are a necessity, send them ahead of time via DHL, FedEx, or another carrier that guarantees two-day or next-day service. Using express services is still no guarantee the documents will reach your room.

PREWEEK PREPARATIONS

I arrived in Tokyo on a Sunday and thought I would spend the day reviewing financials and reports regarding the companies I was going to visit early in the week. My assistant had sent them to the hotel the Wednesday before, but the materials had not arrived. Monday night, Tokyo time, I reached my assistant. She tracked down the package down—it was sitting in Customs—and that's where it remained weeks after I returned to the States.

Another time, I was staying at one of the best hotels in London; my FedEx package was set to arrive on a Friday. I reached the hotel on a Sunday—no package. The hotel checked its mail log and had someone check the mailroom—no package. I spent the day reconstructing as much of the information as I could on dial-up Internet; it was pretty slow going. On Monday the package reached my room. It had been delivered over the weekend, but no one at the hotel had recorded it in the logbook.

The following "rules" come from years of arriving at meetings without lost presentation books, derailed preparation materials, and missing notes:

- Stay at a hotel with a business center.
- Leave an extra copy of the material with your assistant.
- Send the material a week in advance and track the package.
- Call the hotel to make sure the package has arrived, and that it knows to hold it for you.
- Record the name of the person who acknowledged the arrival of the package, and the name of the hotel personnel who will be responsible for delivering the package to you when you arrive.
- Save the information on your office computer and a portable one, if you are taking one.
- If you intend on taking notes longhand, carry your notebook or pad with the questions that you have prepared ahead of time. Don't entrust that to the mail.
- If you are making a presentation, carry at least one hard copy and a CD (or thumb drive) so that your presentation can be replicated if all of the books haven't arrived.

Copy Passport Pages

Make copies of the first two pages of your passport to carry in a different place than that in which your original is stored. In addition, leave copies with someone you trust in case you need them faxed to you at your destination.

Copy Wallet Contents

This is a great time to empty your wallet of everything you do not need on the trip (your Pizza Hut coupons, for instance), and make sure what you do take is relevant and up to date. You may not need it for the hotels where you are staying, but I suggest carrying your airline card, especially the airline club card, as this may be swiped to generate boarding passes and may be necessary for access to international partners of the airlines you are using.

Store your excess cards in a safe place that is accessible upon your return home. Make a copy front and back of all the cards and information you are taking with you, and make a list of all your account numbers and the vendors' phone numbers.

Back Up the Hard Drive

Back up your hard drive, if this isn't done automatically. Check with your IT department for assistance.

CORSICA

CHAPTER 12: **PREDAY PREPARATION**

> **QUICK GUIDE**
> ❖ Reconfirm all of your meetings, hotels, and transportation
> ❖ Check in for your flight and print your boarding pass
> ❖ Check the weather again
> ❖ Pack

Confirm Your Itinerary

Check your itinerary and reconfirm your hotels and meetings. Airplane equipment, carrier schedules, train routes, and meeting venues can change at the last moment. Rechecking your itinerary can minimize the surprises.

At the very least, you should be able to verify the terminal (and maybe even the gate) where you need to go. Finding the right terminal is not always easy, especially if you are flying on a code-share flight, and the terminal might vary depending on the primary carrier.

Print Your Boarding Pass

For e-ticketed flights, you may be able to retrieve your itinerary, review your seat assignment, check in online, and print out or download your boarding pass by going to your carrier's website and typing in your itinerary number or frequent flyer number and password. Completing these steps can save you time and stress at the airport. You may need to have a ticketing agent or gate agent validate your international documents before you can board. With a boarding pass, you may be able to head straight to security rather than wait until the check-in counters open, which might not be until two hours ahead of boarding.

Some airlines let you download barcoded passes to your cell phone, which can then be swiped for boarding (and security) for domestic flights. It may be worthwhile to see if that option is available for your flights. Print a backup boarding pass just in case.

Check the Weather

Check weather reports for the cities of your first and final destinations, and the intermediate stops as well.

I have been on several two-week trips where I started in Japan with temperatures in the eighties and 100 percent humidity, and ended up in Moscow where there was snow on the ground. This was when wardrobe planning helped. Light blouses, skirts, and sleeveless dresses, along with a wool suit coat, sweater, slacks, a fleece-lined jacket, gloves, and a cap—all in a suit carrier—worked well for the couple weeks.

Packing

Packing Suit Carriers (Lightly)

According to Scott McCartney of the *Wall Street Journal*, over the past decade, twenty-three million passengers in the United States have had bags delayed or lost by major airlines. I strongly suggest using carry-on luggage only: a piece of luggage and a personal item. (Your allowance may be less or more depending on your class of service, regulations of the countries through which you will be passing, and size of airplane.) Your goal when packing is to survive for two weeks with a computer bag and a suit carrier or rollaboard. Unless you're traveling with the same people every day, you can wear your outfits more than once (sometimes your colleagues will do the same). Wash out blouses, shirts, stockings, socks, and underwear, and wear them again. Dispense wrinkles and creases by hanging clothes in the bathroom while showering, or request an iron from housekeeping. If you are lucky enough to stay at the same hotel two nights in a row, use the hotel laundry to stretch your wardrobe another week.

PREDAY PREPARATION

Include in your suit carrier a suit and/or sweater that complements a combination of the following: a dress, a pair of slacks, a skirt, and two blouses. Plan to wear on the plane slacks and a shirt that can be cleaned and worn with your suit. If you are flying in business class, wear a suit jacket that can be given to the flight attendants, along with any other outerwear that can be stowed in the plane's closet and handed to you fresh and unwrinkled upon your arrival.

Typically in a suit carrier there will be a larger pouch, a medium pouch, and a small little zippered area ostensibly used for a garment-bag hook.

Use the large pouch for bulkier objects that are resistant to scratches, such as tennis shoes, power cords, toiletry bags, and anything with Velcro. These items are bulky because they have cavities that are great for storing things. Pack your power cords or roll up your athletic socks and stick them in your shoes. That's also a great place for razors or portable curling irons.

Remember when packing to separate your non-liquid toiletry items that you might need during your flight, such as antacids, aspirin, or earplugs. These can go in your computer bag or briefcase, and should be in easy reach during your flight.

Currently only containers carrying less than three ounces of liquid can be carried on planes in the United States and almost all international flights. All the liquid items must fit in one quart-size Ziploc bag that must be pulled out and placed in a bin in the security line. Storing this bag in the outside pouch of your carry-on makes it easy to access.

The medium-sized pouch is for your underwear, hosiery, and workout clothes. Pack thin panty liners to make underwear easier to clean. When deciding which workout clothes to take, consider 1) the weather you will be experiencing, 2) availability of hotel workout rooms, and 3) the cultural expectations for women's dress in your destinations. If possible, throw in an extra T-shirt or shorts to wear while your workout clothes are being cleaned, or just to have something clean and comfortable to wear around your hotel rooms.

The small, zippered pouch is an excellent space to store a money clip with an extra ID, extra money, and alternative credit card.

Packing Rollaboards and Computer Bags

I prefer using suit carriers for my trips in order to minimize wrinkles, but if that is not your preference, you may want to use rollaboards. Packing rollaboards, utilizing the "bundle-wrapping method" makes good use of your luggage. As described at www.onebag.com, this involves wrapping clothes around a core pouch filled with soft articles such as socks or underwear.

When packing a computer bag, store your computer horizontally, which will give you room to tuck a small purse (assuming you carry one, although it is not necessary) that could include your wallet, small comb, and an extra pen.

The document side of the computer bag is a good place for a copy of the presentation, a notebook for taking notes, and one or two FedEx pouches and corresponding international waybills with your company's international FedEx number in the "Bill Sender" field. (FedEx might not be the preferred carrier in the countries you are visiting. Check at the hotels where you intend to send materials to see what they use.) This section of the bag is also a good place to store a couple of paperbacks or an electronic book reader, if that is your pleasure. There might be special slots on the face of one of the dividers for pens and pencils; fill them with at least two pens and one pencil with a good eraser.

If there is another full-sized zipper compartment, use this for your travel documents: the folder with your itinerary, confirmations of your hotel, appropriate maps, your tickets, and another document carrier with your passport and some extra cash.

Usually there is a slightly smaller zippered pouch with little pockets. These pockets are perfect places to store your iPod, business-card carrier (include five cards for every meeting), a small bag with any drugs you might need on the plane (prescription medication, cold pills, aspirin, stomach and diarrhea medicine), cell phone, and adaptors for your power cords. This pouch is a good place to put a couple snacks, such as crackers, nuts or cereal bars. You never know when you might miss a meal and need them.

Finally, squirrel away in your luggage something that reminds you of home. I like to take a picture of my dog and cats. When I first started to travel, I kept several pictures in an envelope. Now I save a photograph as the background on my computer.

My husband e-mailed me a picture of our newest adopted tabby, poised comfortably on our Caribbean-patterned love seat, staring regally into the camera with vibrant green eyes. I saved the photograph as the background on my computer, and all over the world it popped up on the screen when I booted up, much to the delight of flight attendants, young children, and sometimes adults sitting by me on planes.

One evening my flight was delayed, and the pilot told us we had lost the reverse thrusters but were going to fly anyway. They weren't really necessary when we were going to land in Atlanta. I had watched the pilot talk to the mechanic, and when he wasn't satisfied with the answers, he got out and inspected the plane himself. I had confidence in him.

Sitting next to me, an older couple were heading out to their dream vacation in Europe with a stopover in Atlanta. They were worried about missing their connection, but the gentleman was more worried about the safety of the flight, and asked me several times if they should take a different plane.

"I've watched this pilot. If he didn't think it was safe, he would say 'no go,'" I said.

The man nodded, and the couple decided to stay, but before they made us turn off our electronics, he had one last request. "Let's see the kitty again." All of us made it safely to Atlanta.

ID Your Belongings

Even if you are not checking luggage, you will want to ID your luggage and electronics with something more substantial than the little tie tags they give you at the airport. You may want to tape a business card on electronics, and slip one in the manufacturer's provided baggage tag. I also include in my luggage my frequent-flyer luggage tag, so if outside IDs are ripped off, the luggage can still be identified.

After you have everything packed, lift your luggage and walk across the room. Can you carry it without difficulty? Congratulations if you can. If not, take out clothing you don't need. Remember, you can always wash things out in the sink.

Once you have everything balanced and ready, set everything in the same place and set your alarm.

Forwarding Luggage

For a fee, you can have luggage delivered to your destination, which frees you up from lugging bags during the trip, and/or collecting them afterward and escorting them through Customs. According to luggageforward.com, charges are based on luggage category, travel distance, and service level. In addition to the quoted charge, other items to consider when selecting this service are:

- additional fees
- packaging of items
- locking luggage
- disallowed items
- insurance coverage
- warranties
- estimated delivery times
- willing recipient

When traveling abroad, plan for the luggage to arrive at least the day before you leave home. If delivery is delayed, you can still carry on necessary items.

American Airlines contracted with a third party to offer this service in 2012 for domestic flights and flights originating from very select international ports. It will be interesting to see if other airlines offer similar or expanded services.

CHAPTER 13: **FINAL PREPARATIONS**

> **QUICK GUIDE**
>
> ❖ Monitor your flight
> ❖ Confirm possession of credit card, passport, coat, and ticket.

Reconfirm Your Flights

Phone the airline or use its website or app to make sure your flight is on time. If there appears to be a significant delay, especially one that could compromise making your connections, or if the flight is canceled, call the airline right away to see if you can be rescheduled on alternate flights.

Check the Essentials

Check one more time to make sure you have a credit card, passport, coat, and tickets. You can go almost anywhere with those four items.

In 2004, Hurricane Jean was heading for Florida, and my house was declared in an evacuation zone days before I was starting an around-the-world trip. There was great risk that air travel originating in South Florida was going to be interrupted, which threatened my ability to catch my Atlanta-to-Tokyo flight, the beginning of a tightly choreographed two-week trip.

To catch the Atlanta-Japan flight, I had to leave South Florida a day early, but I could not get back to my house before doing so. Luckily, I always carry my passport, so I picked up an outfit from the dry cleaner's, took my credit card to the mall, bought a suit, and purchased all the toiletries I needed for the trip at a drugstore. When it came down to it, all I needed for a two-week trip was a credit card and a passport.

Zip and Button

Check the zippers, snaps, and buttons on every bag, case, and item of clothing so that nothing falls out.

Walking through the Fort Lauderdale and Atlanta airports, I caught a couple of glances thrown my way and thought that my intensified workouts were paying off. A pay phone where I was headed was blocked by a handsome man with a wolfish smile. He made room for me to slide next to the adjacent phone while I set my computer bag on the nearest row of chairs.

Finishing my call, I turned away from the phone and bent over to stow my wallet.

"Miss, excuse me, miss!"

Annoyed, I turned around to face Mr. Wolf Smile.

"Sorry to bother you, miss, but did you realize your skirt is unzipped?"

Never leave your house, car, hotel, airplane, or toilet stall until you make sure everything—I mean *everything*—is zipped.

Hug Your Loved Ones

Remember how everyone looks at you before you leave the house, as they wonder where you are going away, once again. Think of how happy they will be to see you back home.

PARIS, FRANCE

CHAPTER 14: **AIRPORT CONSIDERATIONS**

> **QUICK GUIDE**
> ❖ Check in
> ❖ Clear passport control and security

Check In

If you have not checked in online, try the airport kiosks. You will be required to swipe a credit or airline card, or enter your itinerary number and scan your passport.

If you are unable to use a kiosk, and you are in the United States, proceed to the international ticket counter of the airline you are flying. In airports outside the United States, check flight boards displayed at various places in the terminal to see which check-in counters to use for your flight. On long flights, there may be separate business and first-class check-in lines that are not contiguous to coach check-in. Sometimes those are listed on the flight boards or you may have to ask.

On a recent flight from Japan to the United States, I was unable to find the business-class check-in line. When I asked an agent at the front of the check-in line where to go, the agent slid me in front of the coach queue, and did so for other business-class passengers as well.

Check-in is a good time to confirm your seat selection (up/down, aisle/window, front/back) and request access to a club lounge if you are traveling in business class or higher, if you have a club room membership with the airline you're flying on or a partner airline, or if you have a certain credit card. If you do have access, you may be granted a pass for your time at the airport, or permitted to use your membership card. After confirming access, ask where the club is located, how far it is from your gate, and if it's before or after security.

Passport Control and Security

In the United States, the check-in counter usually doubles as passport control. In other countries, your documents will be reviewed and exit papers collected by immigration authorities. (In Japan, part of your entry document is stapled to your passport.)

After going through passport control, you might head directly to security for the whole terminal or security will be at the gate. Compare the concourse number and gate of your flight on your boarding pass with overhead signs to make sure you are entering the correct concourse. There may be a special line for business or first class. Check your pockets and store phones, coins, or metal objects in your carry-on.

You may have to show your passport and boarding pass again before entering the security line, or present both while going through the line. Once you reach the X-ray machine, do the following:

➢ Pull out your laptop and any video equipment (and electronic notebooks without cases) and place them in a bin on the conveyer belt. Hook to this tray, or place separately on the belt or in another bin, your shoes and belt.

➢ Put into the same or separate bin any jackets, suit coats, bag of liquids, and metal objects you have forgotten to stow.

➢ Do not place your boarding pass or passport on the conveyer belt unless instructed, as security personnel might examine them after you move through the detector and before you pick up your belongings.

You might be requested to enter a scanning machine, where you're required to stand and position your arms and legs. If you elicit a response from the machine, security may ask you to stand aside while they run a wand over your clothes. In some instances, they will send you to a booth, where you are patted down by security personnel of your same sex. The whole process may seem quick or lengthy and daunting. In any case, remain calm, do as instructed, and do not under any circumstance make any incendiary comments or jokes about bombs, guns, or hijacking. In many countries, rudeness or improper language can subject you to further search and delays or even an arrest.

After you go through the scanner, pick up everything from the belt and put it on or in the correct bag. If the area is congested, move to the side to put on your shoes and clothes. Before you leave the security area, make sure you have all of your belongings, especially your passport and boarding pass. On an international flight, you may need to show both before boarding the plane. After security, you can stop off at the lounge if you have time, or go directly to the gate. Typically, transcontinental flights board forty-five minutes to an hour before takeoff. If you are not at the gate thirty minutes before takeoff, you could lose your seat.

LONDON, ENGLAND

CHAPTER 15: **SAFETY AND CONVENIENCE**

QUICK GUIDE

- Assure your room's safety
- Learn your evacuation routes
- Vet all visitors
- Secure valuables
- Carry your key, ID, and money when out of the room
- Apprise a friend of your itinerary

At the Hotel

Room Escort

Even if you can carry your own luggage, accept the bellhop's offer to escort you to your room. Before you enter your room, make sure you are happy with the location. Is it too close to an outside doorway, ice machine, elevator, gym, or bar? If so, go back to the front desk and request another room.

Once in the room, check the bathroom and closets to make sure they are empty, and encourage the bellhop (whom you should tip) to explain the phone, TV, and air conditioning systems if anything looks unfamiliar. Look out the window. Is the room too close to the parking lot or otherwise vulnerable to intruders? Does the room smell bad? Is it clean? You can always try to change your room later, but it is easier to make a change now before you start to unpack.

Room Entrance

Once alone, shut the door and engage the deadbolt. Unless you are awaiting more luggage or correspondence, place the DO NOT DISTURB sign on the door, or engage the corresponding button on the wall or the phone.

In my very first trip to Paris, I took a walk down the Champs-Élysées while I waited for my room to be cleaned. When I arrived back at the hotel, the doorman delivered the wrong luggage. After the right luggage was delivered, I dragged myself into the shower. I walked out of the bathroom to find a man with a clipboard standing in the middle of the room. I had forgotten to engage the deadbolt and the man checking the minibar had used his passkey to access the room. Thank goodness I'd donned a robe before leaving the bathroom.

This would be a good time to set your alarm clock and test the alarm. Set a backup alarm as well, either on your cell phone or with the hotel operator, or both.

Evacuation Route

On the back of your hotel-room door, there will be display of the room's rate, hotel liability, and an evacuation route. Note carefully the location of the stairways and exits (you will not be able to use elevators during a fire alarm). Count the number of doors between your room and the exits. Confirm the exit locations the next time you leave your room.

Emergency Lighting

Many hotels provide flashlights or candles in case of emergency. Look around your room—in closets or bed stands—to see if these are provided. Check with the front desk if you can't find any.

Proper Unpacking

Unpacking correctly keeps you organized and makes repacking easier. Hang clothes as soon as possible, either in the closet or in the bathroom if they have a few wrinkles.

SAFETY AND CONVENIENCE

Look for an iron or ironing board in the closet, or request one from housekeeping if shower steam is not enough. Utilize the laundry bag in the closet if you need your clothes pressed, and make sure you fill out the directions correctly. Do not put your clothes in the hall. Ring housekeeping to pick them up.

Put folded items and underwear in the same drawer or as close to each other as possible. Don't scatter them around the room. Put valuables that you won't immediately use in the safe. If a safe isn't available, keep them locked in your luggage. Put toiletries in the bathroom but keep them close together. If you have time, hang separately or lay out your clothes for the next day.

Visitor Checks

Use the peephole before opening the door to visitors. Do not let anyone enter your room who you have not invited. Confirm with the front desk anyone claiming to work for the hotel before allowing the person to enter. Collect faxes or mail at the front desk or have them slid under the door. Direct room service to the proper desk or table, but keep the door open and stay close to the doorway. For repair work, secure your valuables and take a walk or move to the lobby, or at least prop open the door and stay close to the exit until the work is finished.

Night Preparation

Make sure windows, doors, and values are secured. Recheck alarm(s), making sure the clock and wake-up times are correct—note the a.m./p.m. designations.

Set a robe or clothes and shoes by the bed in case you have to evacuate. Place on the nightstand away from the door your key, wallet, and passport in case of emergency. Keep a flashlight or candle and matches closer to your key, along with a wet rag for evacuation in smoky hallways. I like to have a bottle of water handy in case I am thirsty in the night, and earplugs in case of noise.

Securing Valuables

Place laptops, excess cash, and/or extra IDs in the room safe, after you have tested it with a password you can remember—but not 0000. At the very least, store laptops in locked luggage. Check any expensive jewelry with the hotel safe at the front desk. Store your key carefully before you leave the room or leave it at the front desk. Even if you are going out with a group or close friend, make sure you take enough money to pay for a cab to get back to the hotel. Take at least one piece of ID and a credit card.

Money, keys, and ID should be stored in an inside pocket or fanny pack. Only carry them in your purse if you feel confident you will not become separated from it. Carry a card with the address of the hotel and your intended destination separate from your key. Carry your phone or make sure it is safely stored. Finally, if you want to discourage hotel staff entering your room while you are out, leave the DO NOT DISTURB sign on your door and the TV on. Then again, if you want that complementary chocolate on your pillow at night, leave the sign off and make sure your valuables are stored.

Outside the Hotel

Carrying Important Items

Whenever you leave the room, carry a key, ID, and money. In many international hotels, the charming large, distinctive keys are too cumbersome to carry. Leave those with the front desk when you leave. Electronic keys also can be left at the front desk.

Keys can be deactivated by a cell phone, so keep them separate. I use a plastic business-card holder, that can be put in a buttoned or inside pocket, to carry around my key, an extra piece of ID, and extra money for when I go outside the hotel room, even to the gym. Do not keep your hotel room number in the same place as your key.

Filing a "Flight Plan"

Inform someone of where you are heading, and with whom you are going in the evenings. It can be the front desk when you drop off your key, the concierge when you reconfirm your address, or a reliable friend on the phone. If you are traveling or meeting with people you do not know well, make sure your dinner dates know that you informed concerned individuals about what you will be doing. They are likely to take better care of you that way.

Traveling Safely

Check with your friends, coworkers, or the concierge to find the best and safest way to reach your destination. The best modes of transportation might vary depending on the time of the day. Maybe during rush hour it is better to take the subway rather than a cab. Perhaps after dark you want to take a cab or even ask for a car service. Typically the concierge can arrange almost anything and give you the best advice.

Monitoring Valuables

Do not leave your passport in your jacket, do not leave you luggage with someone you do not absolutely trust, and keep your purse attached to your body. Better yet, don't use one.

I don't usually carry a purse, but I took one with me on a European trip. After one of my meetings in Paris, I stuffed my materials into my computer bag and sauntered out the door to my waiting car. Before the driver pulled away from the curb, I noticed what I had forgotten. "Wait, my purse! It has my wallet and my passport in it." I jumped out of the car and ran toward the building I had just left only to be met by the handsome head of investor relations strolling down the sidewalk as only a Parisian can, with my petite handbag, safe and sound.

Once again in Paris, my colleague went out to dinner with clients. He returned to his chair at around 1:00 a.m.. He put on his jacket that had been over the chair, and reached for his wallet. It was missing. Someone had lifted his wallet, which, in addition to containing money and most of his cards, held his green card, and passport. He had a credit card and borrowed enough money to get back to London, where he had to stay until he could replace his documentation. It took a long time.

Once again in Paris, at the train station, my colleagues loaded our luggage into a stack to be watched by our concierge while we all went off in different directions. Most of us came back in a timely fashion to pick up our luggage and make the train. Our escort walked over and tapped the shoulder of one of the stragglers. When the escort turned around, one of the briefcases was missing. Someone had walked past and picked it up.

Remember, always keep anything you cannot afford to lose next to you.

Using Toilets

Bathrooms and toilets differ from country to country, and even within countries. A couple of pointers while utilizing facilities abroad:

- ➤ Carry coins and tissues. You may have to pay to enter the toilet stall or buy toilet paper, assuming it's available.
- ➤ Carry hand sanitizer. Avoid using your hands while eating until you get access to soap and water.
- ➤ Check the seat to make sure it's dry.
- ➤ Especially in Asia, look in the stall before entering to see if it's a Western bathroom with toilets, or a lined hole. If you are in an office building, hotel, or restaurant, ask for the location of the Western bathrooms.

- ➢ If you can't find a Western bathroom, try to use the facilities as carefully as possible or remove clothing items when possible so as not to soil them.
- ➢ Check the floors before entering stalls. In some countries, regardless of the facilities, people urinate on the floor and a custodian mops up afterward.

Tipping Properly

Tipping abroad is a combination of acknowledging the cultural norms, rewarding good service, and avoiding insulting behavior. The cultural norms vary from country to country, and evolve over time. In many countries, tips are already included in your restaurant bill. Generally speaking, tipping 10–15 percent at restaurants, one to two dollars per bag for porters, and 10–15 percent for taxi drivers will work in developed markets (except in Japan, where no tipping is expected). It's less in emerging markets, but you should confer with a guidebook or a local reference person to refine these rules. A great source for tipping abroad is Magellan's worldwide tipping guide, which can be found at www.magellans.com. The amount you tip is important, but so is discretion while tipping.

I am fortunate enough to have access to executive lounges in chain hotels that reward frequent stays. In these lounges, you also may have access to a free breakfast in the morning, light lunches, heavy appetizers in the evening, alcoholic and nonalcoholic drinks at certain times, snacks all day long, and impeccable service. The attendants in the lounge work early in the morning to late at night, and they make sure it is well stocked and clean. Tips are not expected, and many customers don't tip, but usually at the end of my stay I will tip the attendants twenty euros. It has always been graciously accepted, and I am remembered when I revisit and receive great service. I consider it a good bargain.

LUZERN, SWITZERLAND

CHAPTER 16: **HEALTHY TRAVELING**

> **QUICK GUIDE**
> - Eat carefully
> - Exercise frequently
> - Rest well
> - Wash your hands often
> - Avoid unsafe food

Eat Well

When I first started traveling internationally, I enjoyed all the snacks and deserts I was offered in business class on planes, airport lounges, and hotel clubs. I enjoyed experimenting with foods and wine from room service, and sharing great meals with clients. Six months after I started traveling, I went back to the doctor for my yearly checkup. I had gained five pounds! The actual amount was not alarming as much as how fast I gained the weight. He suggested I adjust my lifestyle before the weight gain became a problem. I did start to monitor my food intake, but over the years, modest weight gain continued until it was beginning to become a problem, and I realized that I had to seriously change my traveling lifestyle. I read up on nutrition, talked to my doctor, and some of my fellow travelers. Some of my new habits worked their way into my day-to-day life and the pounds slowly went off.

A few pointers:

- Do not eat every time there is a meal served. It is totally appropriate to refuse meals or at least courses (cheese, appetizer, dessert, etc.) served on an airplane. Do not starve yourself, but you should not feel obligated to eat every time food is offered.

- Do not clean your plate. If you are curious about the different courses, just have a little bit of each dish.

- Eat light but well. It's difficult and even rude to refuse to eat with clients, colleagues, or sponsors, but choose your food and its preparation carefully.
    - Have a salad with lots of greens, different types of vegetables, maybe fruit and light cheese. Salads take a while to eat and can be filling. If it's an entrée salad, add some fish, chicken, or shrimp. But avoid the bacon, blue cheese, steak, fried food, and creamy dressings. Keep dressings on the side.
    - Skip the bread and butter.
    - For your entrée, eat red meat sparingly. Try broiled, steamed, grilled, or poached lean meats, chicken, or fish, and plenty of vegetables and light grains. Avoid heavy sauces with cream, cheese, and butter. Ask the waiter about the components of the sauce if you are not sure.

- Fruit is your best choice for dessert, but if you want to try something more exciting, split it with a companion.

Exercise Frequently

My former colleagues and I traveled all over the world. Occasionally we would converge on the same hotel, having flown in from different continents to meet with a client or convene an internal meeting. When arriving at the hotel, we usually found each other at the gym—running on the treadmill, using the elliptical trainer, or lifting weights—intent on fighting jet lag, burning calories, or toning muscle. Sometimes we got together for dinner, but frequently we went to our respective rooms to have room-service salads and prepare for the day ahead.

If this seems unusual, I once walked to the gym at the Hilton at Terminal 4 at London's Heathrow Airport. "Retz? Retz Reeves?" A marketing colleague I had worked with at a previous firm was calling to me. We had been on the road together a couple times a month, and most of the time, in the morning or evening, we would run into each other at the gym. Over ten years later, he had not gained a pound. At least I was still recognizable.

The best way I have found to counteract the impact of jet lag, especially after the fifteen-hour flights to Asia and the two more hours it takes to catch the bus to the hotel and check in, is to get on the treadmill. I might not run the first day after such a long flight, but I will do my best to at least walk a couple of miles. Exercise chases away the lethargy that sets in after a long flight, stimulates my senses, and helps me sleep better at night. I try to exercise every day and sometimes twice a day while I am traveling.

Exercise does not have to be complicated, but here are a couple of tips on how to safely squeeze some in.

- ➤ Before starting any exercise program check with your doctor. Make it part of your pre-trip checkup.

- ➤ Make sure you stretch. It's a great thing to do while traveling.

- ➤ If you are not a fitness-center exerciser, take a walk. Check the weather for your trip to find what type of casual wear you need to pack for walking. You'd probably need comfortable shoes, socks, pants, shirts, and a jacket. At the hotel, ask the concierge for the safest, nicest places to take a stroll then go and explore. Sometimes I ask the concierge to help me map my meetings, and then walk to them if the weather is nice and I do not have too much to carry. (This is another reason why spike heels are not advisable.)

- ➤ Too cold outside? Check out the hotel's gym. The equipment might seem strange but most of the time an attendant will be willing to help. Walking on the treadmill is easiest, but it's fun to check out some of the other equipment, too. In addition, most good hotels have TVs and radios to help you pass the time while exercising.

- ➤ Work out in your room. Do jumping jacks, dance around the room, pile the phone books into a stair stepper, bring exercise bands with you, do sit up or pushups. Just keep moving!

Rest Sufficiently

Spending hours on a plane, changing time zones, and encountering stressful situations can wreak havoc on your body's clock. The quicker you adjust to your new time zone, the better, and on the plane is the best time to start. I usually try to sleep right after the first meal is served, and I ask not to be disturbed for snacks or other interruptions. If falling asleep on a plane is not easy for you, check with your doctor to see if there are any sleep aids you can take to help.

Once you reach your destination, there are other things that can help you adjust to your new time zone.

- If you arrive in the morning and are very tired, take a short nap, but not longer than an hour.
- If you arrive later in the day, stay away awake until regular bedtime for locals. Exercising soon after you arrive or in the early evening can help stimulate your body in the short term and help you sleep later.
- During the trip, avoid staying out too late or drinking too much alcohol.
- Only use sleep aids as prescribed by your doctor.
- Eventually your body will adjust to the new time zone on its own, and a couple nights of truncated sleep will not hurt you in the long run. So do not worry if it takes you a couple days to adjust.

Stay Clean

Every day, but especially when you are traveling, your skin, especially your hands, come in contact with surfaces (keyboards, gym equipment, railings, door handles, airplane pillows) that other people have touched or rubbed against. These items might harbor their bacteria or viruses, which could be transferred to your skin, clothing, or bags. So, while traveling, wash your hands frequently and correctly, especially before eating.

To correctly wash your hands, lather up well, scrub vigorously for twenty seconds, and rinse well so that you dislodge dirt, bacteria, and viruses. The use of antibacterial soap is not necessary. Dry your hands thoroughly, and use a paper towel to turn faucets on and off and open doors.

Washing with soap and water is the best way to disinfect your hands, but if that is not possible, the CDC's consumer reports recommend using an alcohol-based product such as Purell, which comes in travel sizes.

Other recommendations, some of which you can find in *Consumer Reports*, to protect yourself against infections:

- Avoid setting utensils on surfaces that have not been sterilized. Keep them on your napkin or plate.
- Do not touch your face or eyes between hand washings.
- Wipe down gym equipment before and after using it, and take a shower afterward. Put a clean towel over workout mats, and do not share towels.
- Examine your plates, utensils, and glasses before using for leftover food or lipstick.
- To avoid transmitting cold viruses, sneeze into your sleeve or a Kleenex rather than your hands.

Avoid Infectious Diseases

Foodborne and Waterborne Diseases

The World Health Organization notes that "one person in three in industrialized countries may be affected by foodborne illness each year." Although difficult to document, foodborne diseases are higher in the developing world. In many emerging markets, therefore, I avoid eating outside of hotels or high-profile restaurants, I drink bottled water (which I use even for brushing my teeth), avoid ice, and eat only cooked foods.

The World Health Organization (WHO) offers on its website (www.who.int) a more complete list of ways to avoid foodborne and waterborne diseases. Its *International Travel and Health Guide* contains chapters that can be read online or downloaded to your computer.

Other Infectious Diseases

According to WHO, besides the foodborne and waterborne diseases, possible modes of transmission of infectious diseases include:

- vectorborne diseases (transmitted by insect bites)
- zoonoses (transmitted by animals)

- bloodborne diseases
- sexually transmitted diseases
- airborne diseases
- diseases transmitted from the soil

WHO's *International Travel and Health Guide* lists in detail the areas where these diseases are prevalent, the degrees of risk of infection to the international traveler, and ways to avoid becoming ill.

INSTANBUL, TURKEY

CHAPTER 17: **ROAMING ABROAD**

QUICK GUIDE

❖ Explore using trains instead of planes for intercity travel
❖ Understand the risks with renting cars abroad
❖ Compare public transportation, walking and taxis for intracity traveling

---

If transportation is not provided for you within or between cities, you have several options that have tradeoffs between cost and convenience.

Intercity

Planes

Even if you are already abroad and all your flights are ticketed, traveling by plane between cities added to your itinerary can still be done at a reasonable price. Indeed, for long distances, it may be the only feasible option. In order to moderate the impact of the cost, try the following:

95

➢ Check with your travel agents or call the primary (transoceanic) airline to see if you can add a leg to your itinerary without a penalty.

➢ Look online, using Expedia or Travelocity, to see what fares and flight combinations are available for travel between your destinations.

➢ Check your favorite airline websites to see if there are cheaper flights at different times during the day, and check alternate airports around the same city, as some regional airports may be cheaper to fly in and out of.

➢ Check the websites of budget airlines for cheap fares. The Travelers Digest Budget Airlines website has a list of budget airlines grouped by their country of origin, along with a description of the airlines and links to their websites. There may be extra charges for luggage and food on these airlines, but the fare may be worth it.

After planning a trip to Europe, I realized I needed to make a connecting flight from Nice to Paris. The travel agent quoted me four hundred fifty dollars for a coach seat, around noon from Nice to Paris's Charles de Gaulle. I visited Air France's website and found a flight from Nice to Paris's Orly airport just half an hour later for less than a hundred dollars. A little flexibility and searching can yield some nice rewards.

Trains

For going between cities or major stations within cities, trains are a convenient, relatively inexpensive and enjoyable way to travel in the developed world. Usually you can arrange train transportation through your travel agent or hotel concierge, but, especially in Europe, it's easy to make and manage reservations and even pick your seat online. For Europe, my favorite website is Rail Europe®. This website gives you all the different options and various classes, both connecting and direct, between the cities of your choice. Note whether the fair you choose is refundable, which is usually a more expensive option, but if you are not sure of your itinerary, you may want the flexibility of exchanging tickets. Also, even in Switzerland, trains are not always on time, and stations can be big and complex, so leave enough time to make your connections. I suggest at least forty-five minutes.

If you are taking several train trips, consider a multiday or multicity train pass. Once you buy a pass, you may still want to book a reservation and/or reserve a seat (for an extra charge) when you are sure of what train you want to take. You may also buy a single country pass that permits access to the city's entire public transportation system.

An additional website for information on traveling on railways all over the world is www.railserve.com. Just click on the "Passenger Rail, Transit & Train Travel" link to the region you are interested in. For instance, for information on riding the subway in Japan, click on "Passenger Rail, Transit & Train Travel—Asia" and then select "Tokyo Metro." (This page is sorted alphabetically by city, railway, and station combined, so you might find more specific information by clicking on different selections.) You will then have access to information on buying tickets, sightseeing, and using the subway in Tokyo.

Rental Cars

Unless you are very familiar with the road systems and laws of the country you are visiting, I would not recommend renting a car abroad. But if you do decide to rent a car, here are some considerations courtesy of Best Car Rental Tips (www.best-car-rental-tips.com):

- The minimum age to rent a car is twenty-five, unless some countries let you pay an underage fee. There are maximum ages for renting a car in some countries as well.

- Many international countries will charge fees for extra drivers and require proof of credit (debit cards might not be enough) for designated drivers.

- Rental car insurance coverage may include: airport fees, VAT (value added tax), public liability, or mandatory insurance coverage. Check with your credit card company to see if they cover nonmandatory insurance. Check with the policy you bought or is provided by your credit card to establish what is covered and what the deductibles are.

- US and Canadian driver's licenses are accepted in most countries, but obtaining an International Driving Permit (IDP) is highly recommended, as it is recognized in over one hundred fifty United Nations members. More information can be found at www.idlicense.com.

- Rental cars abroad are often stick shifts. Communicate directly with the pickup agency if you require an automatic. In the United States and abroad, renters report incidents where they're charged for damage done to the rental car days after their return, even when they are not responsible for the damage. Gary Stoller, a business-travel expert from *USA today*, recommends the following:

- o At pickup, review the car for damage before you leave the rental lot, and make sure an attendant signs off on any damage you see.
- o When dropping off the car, look it over for any damage, and again, have an attendant sign off on the car's condition, especially if nothing is found.
- o If there is no attendant handy, take photos of the auto.

Intracity

Trains/Metro/Subways/Buses

Many international cities have a network of major train lines to take you to and from the airport, suburbs, and across town. At major stops, you can switch to secondary lines, subways, metros, and other forms of transportation to take you to other connecting stops or close to your destination.

On your destination city's website, you might find the best combination of trains/subways to use to get from one place to another. For instance Paris Maps Central (http://parismap.metro-passes.com/paris-metro-map) will give you a very comprehensive plan for getting around Paris. There is also an app for that.

Google Maps[4] (http://maps.google.com) is also a great way to plan an intracity trip. Once at the website, choose the city in which you are interested, select "Get Directions," type in a landmark or address of where you will be starting in the "A" box, and in the "B" box, type your destination. For most cities, a map will appear on one side of the screen with a projected route, and on the left side of the map a route will be detailed. Depending on the city, you may ask for the route to be outlined for car, walking, and public transit. A time for each leg of the route will also be listed to further fine-tune your trip.

Taxis

Taxis can be convenient, if expensive, cross-town transport vehicles, especially when the weather is inclement. If you are burdened down with luggage or other materials, or if you don't feel safe with other means of transportation, taxis might be the fastest way of getting from one place to another.

Obtaining a taxi might not always be easy, however, and you should plan this into your transport time, and include the procedure for hailing a taxi in a discussion with the concierge at the hotel. It is important to understand, for instance, that in some large

---

4

cities you can hail a taxi on the street, but in places like Paris, you can queue at a taxi stand or call for a taxi from your last meeting.

Considerations include:

- How long does it usually take to get a taxi at the hotel at the time you are traveling?
- Will there be taxi stands at your destination?
- What will be the approximate duration of the ride (i.e., how bad is traffic?) at the time you are traveling?

On Foot

If your hotel is centrally located and your meetings or destinations are close by, walking may be the best option, considering both cost and convenience for going between some or all of your meetings. You can download most city maps from the Internet—MapQuest or Google Maps are my favorite sites—before or during your travels. Maps may also be available from the front desk or concierge. The concierge might be a good place to stop by in any case, in order to find out the safest routes to walk, or places to avoid depending on the time of day you are traveling.

In any case, *look in both directions* when crossing streets. In countries where driving is on the left side of the street, you need to look left to avoid getting hit. Also, one-way streets and detours create traffic patterns that intersect first with traffic coming from the left. Finally, nonmotorized traffic (bikers, walkers, animals) has to be accounted for when crossing the street.

Avoid using your phone or texting while walking. In some places it is illegal to do so. Texting and walking is dangerous since you will lose track of your surroundings, your reaction time will be slowed, and you become vulnerable to thieves and errant bicycle riders.

HONG KONG

CHAPTER 18: **OTHER TRAVEL CONSIDERATIONS**

QUICK GUIDE

- ❖ Keep documents safe
- ❖ Remain courteous
- ❖ Monitor travel interruptions
- ❖ Implement a backup plan
- ❖ Enjoy your downtime

Safeguarding Business Documents

While traveling, you will accumulate presentations, notes, little souvenirs, and other documents. Help yourself keep track of everything, while not having to break your back or buy a new suitcase.

Take notes in a notebook, not on handouts or presentations. If appropriate, type notes on your computer during the meetings. This will make following up so much easier.

ADVICE FROM A BROAD ABROAD

> If you do not need to use your computer while traveling, you may be able to save reports and reference materials on flash drives that can be plugged into a computer at the hotel's business lounge. (Charles Yu of *USA Today* recommends you make sure ahead of time that this is available.)

> Ask for presentations to be e-mailed or mailed to you, or send them back yourself by international carriers such as DHL or FedEx, or have the hotel mail them for you. Find out the account number of your firm's various couriers so that you can charge shipping charges directly to the firm. Never ship your notebook or computer, unless it needs to be repaired. Presentations are replaceable; your thoughts are not.

> Keep track of your receipts in one place, either in a large envelope or folder. Put in there hotel bills; receipts for taxis, food, drinks, and paper products; and even the less obvious ones, such as foreign-exchange receipts, when you are charged a transaction fee. There's no reason you should have to pay that. Or take photos of receipts with your smartphone and print them upon your return. According to Nancy Trejos of *USA Today* organizing receipts is important for tax records of self-employed individuals, or those who are not reimbursed for all expenses. Indicate on your receipts the reason for the expense and with whom you met. Keep your travel documents (passports, tickets, etc.) in one folder or pouch in the same part of your luggage at all times. That way, you can easily check them, which you should, every time before you leave a venue.

Common Courtesies

> If you want to be invited back, be a gracious travel companion or guest.

> Be aware of the cultural differences of your destination. If you have not had time to research your destination, ask your hosts or the hotel concierge about any unusual customs endemic to that region that would be wise for you to follow.

> Show up on time. Don't make others wait for you. Whether you're meeting your travel companions, company management, or driver, remember their time is valuable, too.

> Keep up with the group. Do not put colleagues in the position of keeping track of you.

OTHER TRAVEL CONSIDERATIONS

➢ Take care of yourself. Do not make others carry your stuff, fetch your coffee, answer your phone, or watch your bags (unless that is their assignment). You are responsible for your own belongings.

➢ Don't whine. If there are issues or problems, deal with them. Do not bring everyone else down.

➢ When appropriate, offer to share expenses. You can always ask for two receipts if you plan to turn in your share for reimbursement.

Canceled/Postponed Flights

You may experience canceled or postponed flights and miss your connections. In that case, proceed to the help or correspondence desk, or ask personnel at the gate for assistance. If there are long lines, call the airline or use the airline app to be rebooked. Most of the time, the airline will have anticipated your delay, and rebook you and your luggage on the next flight available, and give you a new boarding pass. Call whoever was supposed to pick you up and let the person know your new time of arrival, which the person may already know if s/he has been monitoring your flights. Ask the airline staff for reimbursement for meals, phone calls, or overnight accommodations. Depending on regulations in the country you are traveling, the airline may or may not be required to compensate you.

If it appears that there is too much delay with your rebooked flight, and you will miss a critical connection or meeting, explain your situation and ask the agents if they can assign your ticket to a different carrier with better flights. In this case, a call to your travel agent might be helpful, as you can have the alternative plans in hand.

Depending on your firm's travel policy, if you must catch an earlier flight than the one on which you are rescheduled, and the airline will not reassign your ticket, ask your travel agent to book you on the alternate carrier's flight and credit back the unused portion of your ticket. You could book on the other carrier yourself, but you might lose the rest of your itinerary on your primary airline.

Airport Closures

Airport closures due to weather, strikes, natural disasters, or other reasons can be major disruptions to travel. When an airport closes, flights are usually canceled for that day because inbound planes can't land. When travel is resumed, travelers who have assigned seats on that day's flights have priority over those whose flights were canceled.

This means it can be days before you are rebooked on another flight, and it may be on a lesser class of service.

If you are scheduled to fly out on a future date when it's likely the airport will be open and you are not in any danger, don't change your flight, just monitor the situation.

If around the day of your international flight, you discover that the airport is closed or the airline is ceasing flights or shutting down, get a hotel room for the night, by the airport if possible. Maybe you won't need it, but it's better than spending the night on the airport floor.

Call the airline to see if you have been rescheduled. Volunteering to fly on more convoluted routes with more stops, or taking a train to another boarding point might help you get an earlier flight out or keep your class of service.

If you are not satisfied with the rebooking, or if you feel you are in danger, call your travel agent. Depending on your company's travel policy, your agent may be able to get you out on a different airline or boarding point.

Savoring Downtime

While traveling, I tend to spend almost all of my downtime exercising, sleeping, or getting ready for my next day's meetings. On my international trips, however, I sometimes end up on a weekend with two long days in the same city.

Even I can only work so much, and I have found that taking a break for a couple of hours on weekends to explore my adopted city or town refreshes the soul and the mind, and allows me to appreciate the wonderful world we live in.

Hopefully you had time before you left home to research the city that will host your layover, or at least popped in your bag a guide with suggested things to do. If not, ask the concierge or front desk for a guide, a detailed map of the city, and some advice.

Take a Walk

The easiest way to familiarize yourself with your city is to take a walk! Using your map and perhaps advice from the hotel, point yourself in a direction and take a stroll. In this rather casual fashion, I have enjoyed:

> ➢ The surprise of a giant sculpture sprouting from the sidewalk in Basel, Switzerland
>
> ➢ The beauty of the lake and the bustle of the Bahnhof railway station in Zurich

OTHER TRAVEL CONSIDERATIONS

- The overwhelming sense of history found on the streets of Madrid and London
- The savoir faire of the Champs-Élysée in Paris
- The sense of community along Queens Necklace in Mumbai
- The spicy scents and riot of colors in Hong Kong.

Visit a Museum, the Zoo or a Park

In many cities, there are interesting local or world-renown museums, zoos, or parks within walking distance or a short cab ride from your hotel.

On one particularly grueling trip, I spent a week in Japan and Hong Kong, and flew over the weekend on the Friday night to Paris, where meetings were scheduled for Monday. I then planned to make my way through Europe before returning to the United States the next weekend.

My body clock was a mess, and I was going stir-crazy in the hotel, so I grabbed a map from the concierge, and took a forty-minute walk to the Louvre. (I could have done it much faster in the Metro.) As many times as I had been to Paris, I never had seen the Louvre. I am so glad I allowed myself the pleasure of a few hours seeing the great sculptures and paintings I had only read about. I even queued to see the Mona Lisa, an image that still burns in my brain. I walked back to my hotel refreshed and feeling just a bit like a Parisian.

Schedule a Tour

Most hotel concierges are quite happy to help you schedule a tour, which can take as little as a few hours or a whole day. For instance:

- From Paris, you can take a bus and tour Versailles.
- In London, you can ride the big red buses, and get on and off wherever you want to visit historical monuments.
- Take the ferry in Hong Kong over to Macau, or take a ride to the top of Victoria Hill.
- Board a train and wind through the countryside and mountains of Switzerland.

Most companies consider weekends the employees' time, even when they are traveling. It is good to use some of this time to type up some notes or prepare for the week ahead, but use some of the weekends to refresh your mind, spirit and body—the work will be there on Monday.

105

Preparing for Customs and Immigration

Immigration Forms

Every individual (or one representative family member) must fill out a US Customs and Border Protection Declaration Form 6059B before you enter the United States. The directions are fairly self-explanatory, but you can reference exact instructions at the CBP website http://www.cbp.gov/xp/cgov/travel/vacation/sample_declaration_form.xml.

These forms should be provided in English and distributed in flight. If English forms are not available and you are not fluent in the language provided, ask for a translation!

Making my way through Customs in Miami after a much delayed trip from Spain, I found myself subject to repeated stops and searches. I finally figured out that on my 6059B form (which was in Spanish, and I was too embarrassed to ask for a translation), I had indicated that my trip was for pleasure, when I was telling all the officers that my trip was for business. They had no choice but to treat me as a potential threat.

Make sure you declare the correct amount of goods as required, and sign and date the form before you get in line at Immigration.

Prohibited Items

In order to protect our environment and our citizens' safety, the United States restricts or limits the importation of many items in such categories as agricultural products, prepared foods, and defense articles. Restrictions may depend on the origin of the product. Disallowed products may not be obvious to the average traveler, so it pays to review the list of unsafe items published by the CBP (Customs and Border Patrol) at the following web address: http://www.cbp.gov/xp/cgov/travel/id_visa/kbyg/prohibited_restricted.xml

Customs

After passing through Immigration, you will collect any checked luggage and pass through Customs. The officer may simply collect your form, or s/he may search your luggage. If you have not properly declared items purchased abroad, you could be subject to import duties, fines, or worse. Prohibited items are subject to seizure.

CHAPTER 19: **TRIP RECOVERY**

> **QUICK GUIDE**
>
> ❖ Reacclimatize
> ❖ Enjoy a celebratory dinner
> ❖ Unpack and take inventory
> ❖ Backup your computer
> ❖ Debrief your colleagues
> ❖ Complete your expense report
> ❖ Update your contacts
> ❖ Look forward to your next trip

Acclimate Your Body

The shock to your body when arriving home is the same as that when arriving in a foreign city that has a six-to-thirteen-hour time difference from your departure city. So it's just as important to get back on schedule once you get home as when you travel. Some steps you can take to help your body adjust:

➢ Try to sleep on the early part of the flight and your body will already start to be in tune with your home time zone.

➢ Exercise when you get home in order to step up your metabolism and feel better.

➢ Eat lightly, avoid alcohol, and drink plenty of fluids on the first day back.

➢ Do not sleep until your regular bedtime.

➢ An extra hour in the sack the next morning is okay, but try to get back to your normal routine as soon as possible.

Celebrate Your Homecoming

Before the trip, I plan a dinner with my family or friends for two days after I arrive back home. The thought of this dinner helps me look past the long flights and nights, when I wonder if I will ever get home. The dinner itself is a great way to immerse myself back into the community and share my thoughts about the trip.

Unpack and Take Inventory

The morning after your return home, empty your bags and take an inventory of your clothes, credit cards, power cords, cell phones, and travel documents. Hang up those clothes that you can wear again. Drop your dirty washables in the hamper and bag up your dry cleaning *after* checking your pockets for receipts, credit cards, and travel documents. Refresh any toiletries that have run down, and put back in their correct pouches your passport, other IDs, and credit cards.

I had to do a quick turnaround after an overseas trip. I dropped my clothes at the dry cleaner's and headed to the airport. When I reached the security line, I could not find my passport in the pocket in my computer bag. As this was a domestic flight, I proceeded through security using my driver's license. As I sat on the plane waiting for it to take off, I realized I must have left my passport in the inner pocket of my jacket. I immediately called my assistant, who ran down the passport before it was ruined by the dry cleaning.

Retrieve Lost Articles

One time, I reached Korea after a stint in Hong Kong and realized I left my workout clothes in a small drawer by the shower. (How many of my own rules did I break there?) I called housekeeping at the Mandarin Hotel in Hong Kong. Someone found the articles I had forgotten (as well as some handouts I purposefully left behind), and sent them to my office in Fort Lauderdale after I provided my corporate FedEx number.

Airlines, hotels, and restaurants all have a lost-and-found section. Most establishments will be happy to reunite you with your belongings, as good service typically means return business. If you think you left something behind, do not hesitate to call to see if it can be retrieved.

If you are missing a personal electronic device, activate the "Find" feature. If you do not find the device, unregister it online or with the respective customer service, and cancel any automatic subscriptions. Review your credit card history online to make sure nothing unusual has been charged. If there is an unusual charge, call the credit card company immediately. If you can't unregister the credit cards linked to your device, cancel them.

If credit cards are missing, review your online statement, let the credit card company know about any unusual purchases, and cancel them. You will get a new card in the mail more quickly than having the old one sent to you. You may have to go over your subscriptions, clubs, and prescriptions and give your provider your new number.

Back Up Your Computer

If you saved any documents on your hard drive during your trip, either transfer them to your company's network or have your computer backed up.

Trip Follow-up

As soon as feasible, summarize the conclusions taken away from your trip and what actions are required to follow up. A quick review might include such observations as:

> Employees in an overseas office feel disenfranchised. Explore a weekly conference call and encourage them to spend some time in the home office.

> A certain chemical company looks interesting. Do more in-depth research to see if it is a worthwhile investment.

> One of the countries visited may be a good place to relocate some factories. Conduct a feasibility study.

Once you have summarized your observations and general conclusion, write up in detail each visit, or block of visits, and recommendations in separate files. The files can be referenced by other employees who are following up on the recommendations, or planning their own visits.

Complete Your Expense Report

The longer you wait to complete your expense report, the more likely receipts for the trip will be misplaced. Most credit card companies allow viewing your bill online, which will have your foreign charges translated into US dollars. This exchange rate can be used for smaller amounts, or you can use the rate printed on your money-exchange transactions. This rate is typically less favorable than the one provided by your credit card company, but may better represent what you paid for miscellaneous expenses.

Reinforce New Contacts

During your trip, you probably made some very good contacts who could assist you in the future or whom you might assist. Drop them an e-mail, or even better, write a note that expresses your appreciation, discusses follow-up action you might be taking, and offers reciprocal assistance in the future.

For others who greatly assisted in planning your trip, organizing your visits, or gathering information, a note of thanks or a bouquet of flowers might be a good way to show your appreciation.

In the meantime, store all of those business cards, preferably electronically, so that you can keep up with your contacts in the future.

Save Your Photographs

If you took pictures while you are traveling, have them developed, print them out, or store them digitally as soon as possible. They will greatly enhance the memories of your trip and are great to share with friends and colleagues. The longer you wait to print or store these photos, the more likely the "film" will be ruined, lost, or photographed over.

Plan Your Next Trip

Somewhere in this trip will be the seeds of another one—a way to finish work you started, explore ideas from a different angle, or head out to new horizons. Even if this trip will not occur for another six months, start planning it now and make it happen!

LIST OF AUTHORITIES

Edward C. Baig, "Amazon Electronic Reader Kindle 2 Is a Nifty, if Costly, Second Act," *USA Today*, February 24, 2009, 4B.

Elizabeth Bernstein, "When It Never Gets Easier to Say Good-bye," *The Wall Street Journal*, September 18, 2012, D3.

Kathy Chu, "Weigh Before You Pay: Debit or Credit?" *USA Today*, Aug. 1, 2008, 3B.

Consumer Search, April 3, 2010, http://www.consumersearch.com/pda-reviews/important-features.

Consumers Union, "Dangerous Bacterial Infections Are on the Rise. What Can You Do to Counter the Trend and Stay Safe," ConsumerReports.org, November 2007. Reprinted July 2012, http://www.businesslife.com/articles.php?id=56403.

Daniel Dumas, "Wired Smart Guide: Know Your Smartphones" *Wired*, June 2009. Web, April 2010, http://www.wired.com/gadgetlab/2009/06/wireds-smart-guide-for-know-your-smartphones.

International Business Center, July 16, 2012, http://www.cyborlink.com/besite/china.html.

Ibid, http://www.cyborlink.com/besite/india.htm.

Ibid, http://www.cyborlink.com/besite/russia.htm.

Ibid, http://www.cyborlink.com/besite/germany.htm.

Ibid, http://www.cyborlik.com/besite/italy.htm.

Ibid, http://www.cyborlink.com/besite/spain.htm.

Ibid, http://www.cyborlink.com/besite/united_kingdom.htm.

Ibid, http://www.cyborlink.com/besite/brazil.htm.

Ibid, http://www.cyborlink.com/besite/africa.htm.

Luggage Forward, Inc., November 15, 2012, http://www.luggageforward.com.

Scott McCartney, "Finding the Best Fares to Europe," *The Wall Street Journal*, June 6, 2012, D1.

Scott McCartney, "Oops! I Forgot My New iPad On the Plane; Now What?" *The Wall Street Journal*, April 26, 2012, D1.

Scott McCartney, "Why Your Bags Aren't Better Off On a Big Airline," *The Wall Street Journal*, September 2, 2008, D1.

Melanie, Pinola, "How to Get 4G or 3G on Your Laptop," *About.com, 2013, Web, http://mobileoffice.about.com/od/wifimobileconnectivity/a/how-to-get-4g-or-3g-on your laptop.htm*

Dennis Schall, "Routehappy Compares Flights," *USA Today*, Oct 8, 2012, 4B.

Gary Stoller, "Lessons from Rental Horror Stories," *USA Today*, July 7, 2009, 3B.

Gary Stoller, "You're Abroad. Disaster Strikes. Now What!" *USA Today*, April 10 2012, 1B.

Nancy Trejos, "Records Crucial When Compiling Business Expenses," *USA Today*, April 3, 2012, 6B.

Nancy Trejos, "Travelers Can Find Friends on the Fly," *USA Today*, May 29, 2012, 1B.

United Nations, World Health Organization, "Food Safety and Foodborne Illness," *International Travel and Health Guide*, www.who.int.

United States, Centers for Disease Control, March 24, 2010, http://wwwn.cdc.gov/travel/content/Vaccinations.aspx.

Ibid, US Customs and Border Protection, *Global Entry Program Information Guide*.

Ibid, Department of State, March 21, 2010, http://travel.state.gov/passport/.

Ibid, http://travel.state.gov/passport/get/first/first_830.html.

Ibid, http://travel.state.gov/passport/forms/forms_847.html>.

Ibid, http://travel.state.gov/passport/get/fees/fees_837.html-fees>.

LIST OF AUTHORITIES

Ibid, http://travel.state.gov/passport/get/first/first_831.html>.

Ibid, https://passportstatus.state.gov/opss/OPSS_Status_c.asp>.

Ibid, http://travel.state.gov/passport/get/renew/renew_833.html>.

Transportation Security Administration, July 21, 2012, http://www.tsa.gov/what_we_do/escreening.shtm.

Rolfe Winkler, "Fighting the iCrime Wave," *The Wall Street Journal*, July 28–29, 2012, C3.

Elizabeth Wise, "The Science of Hand Washing," *USA Today*, January 21, 2009, 6B.

Roger Yu, "Business Travelers Lighten up on Tech," *USA Today*, June 19, 2008, 5B.

Made in the USA
Lexington, KY
18 December 2013